CW00384769

CAMWELL's BIRMINGHAM
One man's transport perspective

Front cover illustration:

One of many junctions we shall encounter in this book where road alterations have transformed the scene beyond recognition, this is Six Ways Aston on 12th July 1949; the underpass and roundabout have swept everything away.

The photograph is taken from the open front balcony of tramcar 343 in Lozells Road. It is following 694 which has already crossed the junction into Victoria Road on its way to Tyburn Road. 604 on service 5 from Gravelly Hill approaches whilst chance has provided a bonus for the photographer with 452 waiting for the junction to clear before crossing from High Street into Birchfield Road bound for Perry Barr.

Tramcar 452, along with sister 451, had long been the oldest in service. Originally constructed as open-top cars in 1903 for the City of Birmingham Tramways Company Limited, they were taken over by the Corporation when the company undertaking was purchased in 1911. The two cars were out of use when taken over but were soon re-trucked and modified before entering service at Arthur Street depot in 1913 for use on the Bordesley Green route. At twenty-five per cent. longer than the Brill cars in use on that route and with five saloon windows compared with three on the Brills they were instantly nicknamed *Titanics* by passengers and staff alike after the large liner of that name which had recently made the news in tragic circumstances. Unusually, the nickname stuck even after further rebuilding with top-deck covers and the cars were still frequently so-called until the end of their lives in 1949.

The remains of the tram tracks curving from Lozells Road and from High Street into Witton Road may be seen. Service 3 which ran between City and Witton via Witton Road was withdrawn in September 1939 but the tracks were retained for departmental use until 1947.

The imposing bank building is that of the National Provincial Bank Ltd which merged with the Westminster Bank Ltd to trade as the still familiar National Westminster Bank [Natwest] as from 1st January 1970.

Back cover illustration:

Steelhouse Lane, taken from the middle of the cross roads of Bull Street and Snow Hill; unless Cam had the co-operation of the point duty policeman, surely a somewhat precarious place to stand in the rush hour. The Lichfield Road services turned at this busy, and in the rush hours congested, terminus where three separate routes all shared the same terminal stub. A Short Heath service is just departing and the next one waits for 554 on the Pype Hayes route to leave so that it can enter the single track. From 1936, Steelhouse Lane became a one-way street northwards but trams were allowed to continue against the flow of traffic.

The building with the clock is the Wesleyan and General Assurance Society and the Gaumont cinema may be seen beyond. On the right, the building with large first floor windows was Grey's furniture store whilst the turreted office block is on the far corner of Upper Priory. Most of this scene was lost under Colmore Circus and the remainder of the buildings vanished in the 1980s. Two other views of the terminus appear on page 83.

CAMWELL's BIRMINGHAM

One man's transport perspective

Edited by Peter Jaques

Birmingham Transport Historical Group

INTRODUCTION

This collection of photographs taken by Arthur Camwell ("Cam") has been assembled by the Birmingham Transport Historical Group as a tribute to one of our founder members.

Although Cam was a prolific photographer whose interests covered the whole of the British Isles, our selection matches the Group's own remit and in this book we confine ourselves to Birmingham, although we confess to stretching the City boundary somewhat in one or two cases where we felt it was appropriate.

Cam was usually concerned to include sufficient background in his transport photographs so that the location could be identified. In view of the myriad changes in Birmingham since these pictures were taken, we feel that they now have an historical interest quite apart from the transport connection for which they were originally taken. We hope that the map on pages 8 and 9 will be of some help in explaining the changes which have taken place.

We make no apology for repeating views which have been published before. In fact, there are very few of Cam's photographs which have not already appeared in print somewhere (not always with proper credit to the photographer). It has only been possible to include a representative selection of his work but we have tried to select those views which have not appeared in print for many years.

The photographs range from 1934 to 1973 but are at their most prolific in early post-war years when the tramway system was being closed down. In later years, Cam turned more and more to ciné-film and there remained less of interest to him in Birmingham particularly as he had all the rest of the country's railways yet to record. In this book we have adopted a broadly chronological approach.

We have also tried to include a few snippets of historical or background detail which we hope will be of interest and while this volume is not the place to give detailed descriptions of the rolling stock involved, a brief mention is given of any unusual features; vehicle numbers which may not always be obvious on the illustration are given where known, for the benefit of those whose particular interest is in such things.

The Group wishes to record its thanks to Geoffrey Claydon for writing the Appreciation, to Paul Addenbrooke, Peter Jaques and Derek Potter whose combined efforts in the selection of photographs and writing the captions is greatly appreciated and to the various copyright holders for their permissions.

Design: Peter Jaques Computer Origination: John A Senior

ISBN No. 978-1-872863-13-9

Published 2007 by
Kithead Limited on behalf of the
The Birmingham Transport Historical Group
21 The Oaklands, Droitwich, WR9 8AD

WILLIAM ARTHUR CAMWELL
An Appreciation

William Arthur Camwell was born on 18th November 1906 in Handsworth, before it was absorbed into the City of Birmingham. Apart from a period of war service, he resided in the Handsworth area for the whole of his life. Never known as William, he was "Arthur" to his older friends but in later years was universally known as "Cam". He was educated at the Central Grammar School in Suffolk Street, Birmingham, leaving it at 17 to work with National Benzole Company. Then in 1924 he joined the Birmingham Municipal Bank, as a junior clerk, and remained with that undertaking until his retirement in 1971. By then he had become the manager of the largest branch of the bank, at Kingstanding.

During the Second World War, in 1942, he was called up for service in the Royal Air Force, transferring to the Royal Indian Air Force in 1943. One of his more memorable tasks was to transport Pandit Nehru, later to become the first Prime Minister of independent India, out of internment with the British. He rose to the rank of Squadron Leader, and his last service posting was as Secretary of the Air Priorities Board in Rangoon, Burma.

Cam's early interests included tennis, cricket and playing the saxophone in a dance band, but gradually his involvement in transport became all-consuming. His interest was fostered at an early age, in travelling to school by train and by the chance factor that the rear windows of his school overlooked the western "throat" of New Street railway station, with its endless movement of Midland and London & North Western trains. He was soon a motorist, his first car being an Austin 7 Tourer, by means of which he travelled all over the British Isles with his bank colleague, Eric Hannan, investigating, recording and photographing tramways and railways.

In 1938 he joined the Light Railway Transport League, later to become the Light Rail Transit Association, an organization which had been established the previous year to lobby for the retention of tramways. He joined others in vigorously pressing for the retention of the Hockley routes prior to their closure in 1939. In the early days of the war he volunteered as an auxiliary tram driver with Birmingham Corporation, working services operated from Witton depot in the evenings and at weekends. In 1941 he became the League's area representative for Birmingham, resuming that position on his demobilization in 1946 and retiring from it in 1957. In 1970 he returned to office as the Association's treasurer, holding this post until 1993.

Cam also served the railway cause through his membership of the Stephenson Locomotive Society. He was secretary of its Midland Branch (later Area) from 1946 until 1993 and Editor of its Journal from 1957 until 1980. In 1979 he was made a Vice-President and held this office until his death. Most memorable was his organising of rail tours, beginning with a trip along the Harborne branch in 1950 and covering many other lines prior to their imminent closure, his last such tour taking place in 1969.

Apart from his interest in trams and trains, Cam also took an interest in motor buses, trolleybuses, aircraft and canals but, inevitably because of his rail commitments, these other transport modes were pursued on a more modest scale. A quiet, unassuming man, he nonetheless possessed a warm personality, coupled with great energy and an infectious enthusiasm. He died on 14th January 1995, after a short illness.

Cam's greatest memorial is his photography of transport subjects. As Dennis Gill remarked in his book *Tramcar Treasury*: "The name W.A. Camwell on a tramway photograph is like the name Royal Doulton on a piece of china". After securing a Rolleiflex camera for the not insignifcant sum of £12 in 1934, he was able to record the transport scene in a manner which few have equalled in atmosphere, clarity and scenic interest. A particular feature of his technique was to capture for the camera not simply the vehicle but the vehicle in its setting, often including a street or a station name as an aid to location. For many years he developed and printed his own negatives, which enabled him to bring out special features, such as overhead wires, by giving the relevant area of the print greater exposure.

In later years Cam turned to colour photography and also became a prolific taker of ciné-films but it is his black and white photographs that demonstrate his genius at its best. It is for this reason that, along with detailed and informative captions, a selection of those photographs which he took in and around his native city, has been chosen by the Birmingham Transport Historical Group as a tribute to him, one of their founder members.

Geoffrey B. Claydon, CB,
President,
Birmingham Transport Historical Group

CAMWELL's BIRMINGHAM

The earliest Birmingham photographs we have been able to trace are a few views of the Harborne branch railway which left the Birmingham and Wolverhampton main line of the London Midland & Scottish Railway Company at Harborne Junction, Ladywood, and ran, with stations at Icknield Port Road, Rotton Park Road and Hagley Road to a terminus at Harborne.

Icknield Port Road station closed on 18th May 1931, having lost almost all of its traffic to the Dudley Road and Ladywood tram services, and by 1934 passenger traffic had diminished further as the bus services along Portland Road, Hagley Road and Harborne Road were more direct. In addition the service was considerably prone to delay where trains joined the main line and really remained attractive only to those living very near to the stations. Closure was announced and the last passenger trains ran on 24th November 1934. Railway season tickets were honoured on the Corporation buses until they expired.

Two days before closure, Cam was on hand to record the scene on Thursday 22nd November as the 12.50pm from New Street to Harborne called at Rotton Park Road Station hauled by an 0-6-2T 6924. One of a class of locomotives designed for suburban passenger traffic by the London & North Western Railway Company, 6924 was new in 1902 and remained in service until the end of 1949.

The Harborne branch remained open for goods traffic until 4th November 1963 when it was closed completely. The bridge over Park Hill Road, Harborne, and the piers of the bridge over the Birmingham Canal at Ladywood, immediately after the branch left the main line, are the most prominent reminders of the line today but many other bridge parapets survive if one knows where to look. The section between Icknield Port Road and Hagley Road was converted to a walkway, though a sadly overgrown and neglected one at the time of writing.

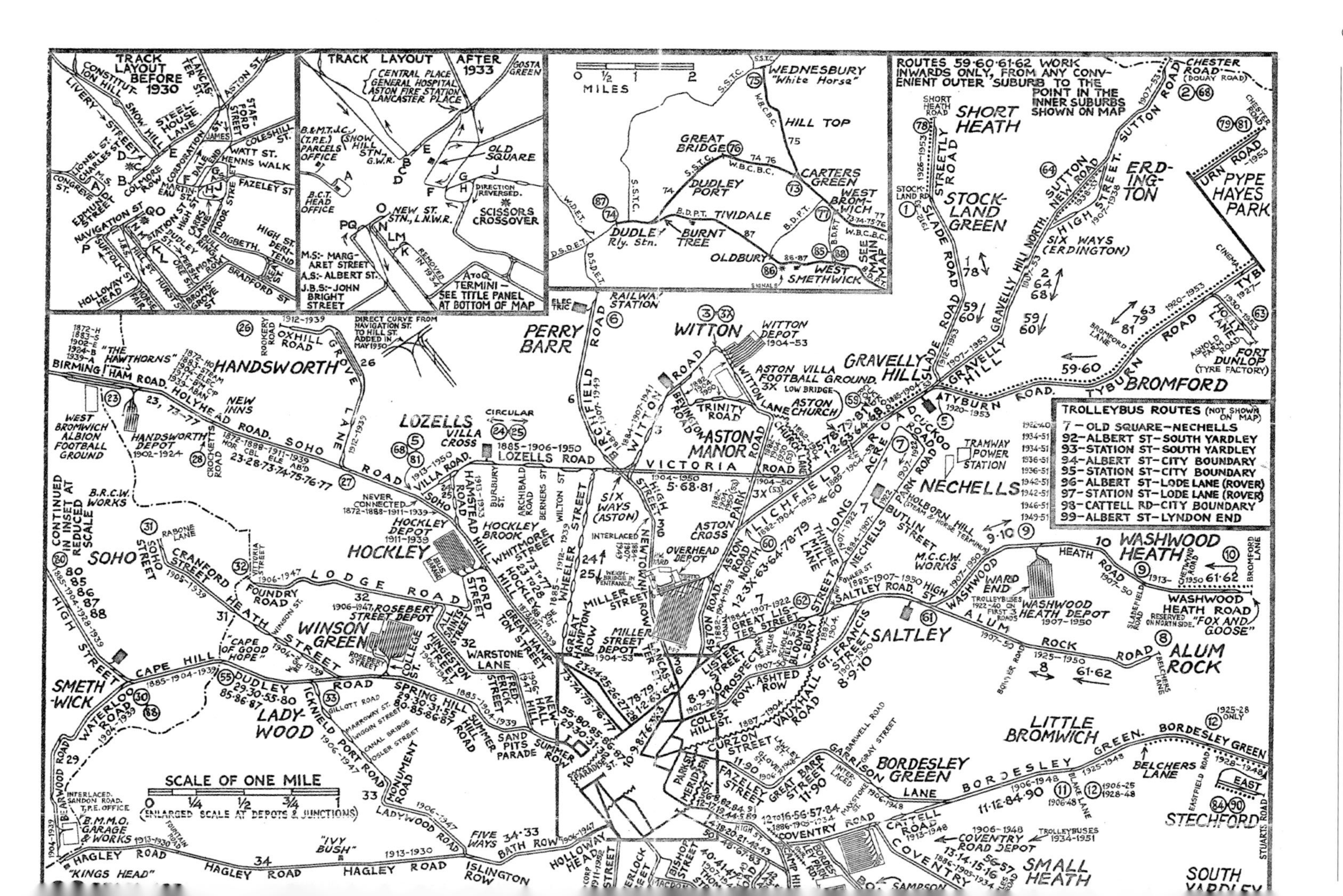
TRACK LAYOUT BEFORE 1930
TRACK LAYOUT AFTER 1933
MILES
WEDNESBURY "White Horse"
HILL TOP
GREAT BRIDGE
CARTERS GREEN
DUDLEY PORT
WEST BROMWICH
TIVIDALE
BURNT TREE
DUDLEY Rly. Stn.
OLDBURY
WEST SMETHWICK
ROUTES 59·60·61·62 WORK INWARDS ONLY, FROM ANY CONVENIENT OUTER SUBURB TO THE POINT IN THE INNER SUBURBS SHOWN ON MAP
SHORT HEATH
STOCKLAND GREEN
ERDINGTON
PYPE HAYES PARK
SIX WAYS (ERDINGTON)
BROMFORD
FORT DUNLOP (TYRE FACTORY)
TROLLEYBUS ROUTES (NOT SHOWN ON MAP)
7 – OLD SQUARE – NECHELLS
92 – ALBERT ST – SOUTH YARDLEY
93 – STATION ST – SOUTH YARDLEY
94 – ALBERT ST – CITY BOUNDARY
95 – STATION ST – CITY BOUNDARY
96 – ALBERT ST – LODE LANE (ROVER)
97 – STATION ST – LODE LANE (ROVER)
98 – CATTELL RD – CITY BOUNDARY
99 – ALBERT ST – LYNDON END
PERRY BARR
WITTON
GRAVELLY HILL
HANDSWORTH
LOZELLS
ASTON MANOR
NECHELLS
WASHWOOD HEATH
HOCKLEY
SOHO
SIX WAYS (ASTON)
ASTON CROSS
WINSON GREEN
SALTLEY
ALUM ROCK
SMETHWICK
LADYWOOD
LITTLE BROMWICH
BORDESLEY GREEN
STECHFORD
SMALL HEATH
SOUTH YARDLEY
SCALE OF ONE MILE
(ENLARGED SCALE AT DEPOTS & JUNCTIONS)
CONTINUED IN INSET AT REDUCED SCALE
"KINGS HEAD"
"IVY BUSH"
FIVE WAYS

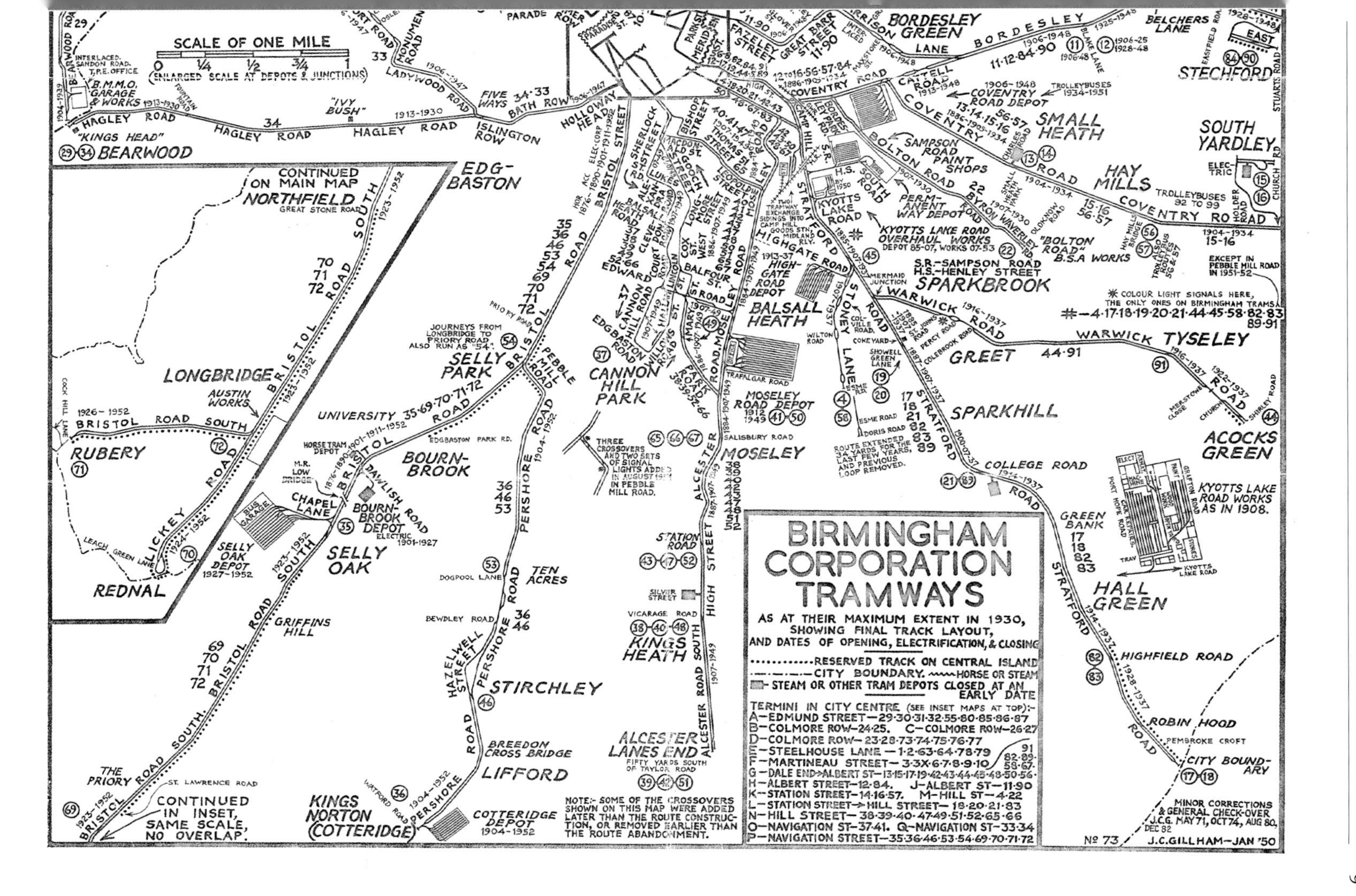
BIRMINGHAM CORPORATION TRAMWAYS
AS AT THEIR MAXIMUM EXTENT IN 1930, SHOWING FINAL TRACK LAYOUT, AND DATES OF OPENING, ELECTRIFICATION, & CLOSING
RESERVED TRACK ON CENTRAL ISLAND
CITY BOUNDARY. HORSE OR STEAM
STEAM OR OTHER TRAM DEPOTS CLOSED AT AN EARLY DATE
TERMINI IN CITY CENTRE (SEE INSET MAPS AT TOP):-
A—EDMUND STREET—29·30·31·32·55·80·85·86·87
B—COLMORE ROW—24·25. C—COLMORE ROW—26·27
D—COLMORE ROW—23·28·73·74·75·76·77
E—STEELHOUSE LANE—1·2·63·64·78·79
F—MARTINEAU STREET—3·3X·6·7·8·9·10
G—DALE END→ALBERT ST—13·15·17·19·42·43·44·45·48·50·56·
H—ALBERT STREET—12·84. J—ALBERT ST—11·90
K—STATION STREET—14·16·57. M—HILL ST—4·22
L—STATION STREET→HILL STREET—18·20·21·83
N—HILL STREET—38·39·40·47·49·51·52·65·66
O—NAVIGATION ST—37·41. Q—NAVIGATION ST—33·34
P—NAVIGATION STREET—35·36·46·53·54·69·70·71·72
NOTE:- SOME OF THE CROSSOVERS SHOWN ON THIS MAP WERE ADDED LATER THAN THE ROUTE CONSTRUCTION, OR REMOVED EARLIER THAN THE ROUTE ABANDONMENT.
SCALE OF ONE MILE
(ENLARGED SCALE AT DEPOTS & JUNCTIONS)
BORDESLEY GREEN
STECHFORD
SOUTH YARDLEY
SMALL HEATH
HAY MILLS
SPARKBROOK
TYSELEY
ACOCKS GREEN
SPARKHILL
GREET
BALSALL HEATH
MOSELEY
HALL GREEN
KINGS HEATH
ALCESTER LANES END
CANNON HILL PARK
EDGBASTON
SELLY PARK
BOURNBROOK
SELLY OAK
STIRCHLEY
LIFFORD
KINGS NORTON (COTTERIDGE)
LONGBRIDGE
RUBERY
REDNAL
BEARWOOD
CONTINUED ON MAIN MAP NORTHFIELD
CONTINUED IN INSET, SAME SCALE, NO OVERLAP.
KYOTTS LAKE ROAD WORKS AS IN 1908.
MINOR CORRECTIONS & GENERAL CHECK-OVER J.C.G. MAY 71, OCT 74, AUG 80, DEC 82
№ 73
J.C.GILLHAM—JAN '50

Above: When the forthcoming conversion of the Stratford Road tramways to motor bus operation was announced, it prompted Cam to focus on Birmingham trams for the first time. The earliest view we can trace is this picture taken on 3rd October 1936. 571 is at Springfield working from Station Street to the City Boundary at Hall Green. The mock Tudor gables of the *College Arms* public house at the junction of Shaftmoor Lane are visible behind the row of houses and shops which are largely unaltered at the time of writing.

One of the reasons given for this tramway abandonment was that there had been so much development on each side of the route that the necessary bus routes to serve the new estates created an over-provision along the main road. Illustrating the point, a Morris Commercial bus on service 32 to Gospel Lane via Lakey Lane is in hot pursuit of the tram.

Above: A note on this print reads 11.55pm 5th January 1937 (7 secs. at f.4.5). The occasion was the final day of operation of the Stratford Road group of routes and the closure to trams of Highgate Road depot. The 11.32pm final journeys from City have arrived at the junction with Stoney Lane, already running ten minutes or so late because of the various ceremonies which had been taking place. Sparkbrook Baptist Church on the right of the picture remains to identify the location today.

It was the Transport Department's practice that last journeys should meet at strategic junctions such as where one of the Circle bus routes crossed so that interchange of passengers could take place. The procession awaiting the inspector's signal to continue is headed by car 173 for Stoney Lane followed by 322 for Hall Green (from Albert Street) and 310 for Acocks Green. Some last buses have interposed themselves before 564 on the final service 18 to Hall Green from Station Street at the rear of the queue.

Replacement bus services for Acocks Green were operated from the garage of that name and the Stratford Road services themselves were run from the recently opened Liverpool Street garage. Conversion of Highgate Road depot was a leisurely affair compared with post-war practice, with the final trams not being cleared out until 5th February, a month after the services ended. The garage re-opened for motor bus operation on 30th June 1937.

Opposite lower: From Stratford Road, a short branch tramway ran along Stoney Lane to terminate outside the Congregational Chapel, that point being the city boundary until 1911. On 2nd January 1937, 120 has reversed at the terminus and waits to return to Hill Street. A school now occupies the site of the chapel but the junction with Esme Road opposite will identify the location. When the trams were withdrawn, there was no direct bus replacement as the Yardley Wood buses which previously ran via Showell Green Lane were altered to run via Stoney Lane.

Above: Taken outside what is now Fircroft College, this scenic view near the top of Griffins Hill in Bristol Road looks towards Northfield. The most striking difference when compared with the scene today is how much the trees have been allowed to grow. The good sprinkling of cyclists and motor-cyclists is also noteworthy. Taken on 19th July 1938, car 334 is working from Longbridge to City

Below: Also on 19th July 1938, in this view of Lickey Road, Longbridge, looking towards City, car 301 is about to cross over and return to City while 305 waits to do likewise. A tram on the Rubery service can just be seen in Bristol Road South behind 301. Note that Lickey Road is not dual carriageway as the dualling was not completed until 1939, although it looks as though some preliminary work is being carried out on the extreme left of the picture

The Bristol Road tram routes were Birmingham's longest wholly within the City. They forked at Longbridge to Rednal or Rubery. This panoramic view **(above)** of the terminal loop at Rednal terminus shows the Lickey Hills in the background and car 746 waiting to leave for City on 19th July 1938. On the same date, 395 is pictured **(below)** waiting to enter the Rubery terminus in Bristol Road South once 372 has left for City. The area is now buried beneath the viaduct of the Rubery bypass and the bank on the left is surmounted by houses. The junctions with Leach Green Lane to the left and Cock Hill Lane on the right are immediately beyond the terminus. There were powers to extend the tramway a further quarter-mile to the city boundary but construction was deferred until the intended Rubery bypass was built. As this did not happen until long after the trams had gone, the terminus was never moved.

Above: This was the Birchfield Road terminus of the Perry Barr route taken from the junction with Wellington Road. The Victorian *Old Crown and Cushion* public house, just visible on the left, was shortly to be rebuilt so that the "old" pub became newer than the *New Crown & Cushion* whose sign can be seen on the right of the tram. The "new" pub no longer trades and the "old" one appears to have become just the *Crown and Cushion.* The Midland Red bus from Walsall leading a line of traffic is just crossing the railway bridge. Taken on 4th March 1938, car 6 is ready to return to City. Even at that date, this terminus could get very congested and there were plans to remove it, either by extending the route just into Walsall Road or curtailing it to near Bragg Road. In the event, neither happened but this is why the picture was taken as Cam has captioned the print "Perry Barr tram terminus prior to removal".

Note the fire alarm pillar on the pavement in the foreground. Commonplace in Birmingham in the days before telephones became so universal, they were painted red and by breaking a glass panel in the box, one could get access to a direct telephone line to the nearest fire station.

Opposite top: This is High Street, Erdington, on 7th September 1938, between New Street and Wilton Road, looking north. On the left car 661 makes for the outer terminus, allowing 675 to enter the single line section which extended almost to Erdington parish church. The open area at the junction with Orphanage Road may be seen behind the trams. The single track became the cause of much congestion when waiting tramcars blocked traffic on what was then the main A38 from Birmingham to the north. Sutton New Road was built to form a bypass and these views were taken to record the old route. The line through High Street closed on 24th September, being replaced from the following day by a line along the new bypass, largely on a central reservation between the carriageways.

Opposite middle: On 22nd September 1938, 688 picks up a good load of city-bound passengers in High Street, Erdington, at its junction with Church Road just south of the single line section mentioned above.

Opposite bottom: A little further north, 666 is at the junction with Orphanage Road, also on 22nd September 1938. The light stone-coloured Britannic Assurance Company building visible in both this view and the one at the top will help to locate them although it is presently Viktor's Drink Store. Overtaking the tram is a Leyland TD4c bus, one of five purchased by the Corporation in 1937 for comparative purposes and seen here on the weekdays only limited stop cross-city service between Erdington and the Maypole operated at that time by Liverpool Street garage.

CUTLERS
WIMBUSH

2
888

2
666

The 71 Class (numbered 71 to 220) trams which dated from 1906/7 were soon to be replaced by 301 Class cars cascaded from Bristol Road. This is likely to be the reason for these photographs but in any case, the Stechford services were intended to be converted to bus operation in 1940 so as to avoid the cost of relocating the tracks when Digbeth and Deritend were made into dual carriageways. The outbreak of war put paid to both road widening and abandonment and so the services survived another ten years.

During football matches at St Andrews, trams were parked on the running line in Garrison Lane and the Fazeley Street service operated single line working between Cattell Road and Maxstoke Street on the outward track from Cattell Road and switching to the inward line on the crossover below Tilton Road. Our **upper** picture is looking east near the railway bridge whilst the **lower** looks westwards near Camp Street. On 24th September 1938, the local supporters will be less than happy when they return as Birmingham City lost to Preston North End 3-1 and remained at the bottom of the Championship League.

Above: Bordesley Green on 24th September 1938 with tramcar 198 loading passengers for Stechford on service 84. Service 12 was a short working to this point and 214 has just reversed here so that the driver was required to register his departure time at the Bundy clock. More of the houses have become shops and where Blake Lane can be seen leading off to the right of 198, the general store is now a Spicy Kebab House.

Below: The Stechford terminus was at the junction of Bordesley Green East with Stuarts Road where car 176 is ready to return to City. The road ahead where the horse-drawn cart is standing was a cul-de-sac named Royston Road. It was to be many years later before it was converted into an extension of Bordesley Green East leading through to Meadway. The distinctive terrace of houses still identifies the location although two of the houses on the left were demolished when the road was widened.

Above: Lozells Road with the *Villa Cross* public house on the left, on 27th September 1938. Car 340 on the Lozells and Gravelly Hill service 5 approaches as 528 waits for departure time on service 24 which ran from City via Wheeler Street and terminated at this point. Until 1933, the Wheeler Street service had been operated as a circular route on weekdays with the Lozells via Hamstead Road service 25. Because it formed part of the Hockley group, the Wheeler Street service was converted to buses in 1939 but the Gravelly Hill service survived until September 1950.
Below: The short connecting link along Hamstead Road between Soho Hill and Villa Road formed part of the Lozells circulars and, after service 25 ended in 1933, was retained for depot journeys between Villa Cross and Hockley. We are looking south on 9th August 1938; the now closed *Roebuck* public house on the corner of Soho Hill is behind the tram and the road name visible in the background marks the beginning of Richmond Road. Cam has persuaded the crew of 514 to display 25 whilst he records the passage of the tram going on to the Wheeler Street 24 service.

Above: Service 5 was usually known as the Lozells and Gravelly Hill route but it actually started in Handsworth at the junction of Villa Road with Soho Road and terminated at the junction of Lichfield Road and Slade Road, just in the road named Gravelly Hill but some distance short of Gravelly Hill the district. The original standard gauge horse tram service between Colmore Row and Handsworth had a branch at this point along Villa Road to Villa Cross and when the Handsworth route was converted to cable operation in 1889 the branch was also converted to the narrower 3ft 6in gauge then becoming standard throughout Birmingham and the Black Country. However, the line was not brought back into use and lay unused until 8th January 1913 when the Lozells service was extended; the junction with the main Soho Road was never reinstated.

The large sign on the tram standard reads "Special buses leave here for Villa Park about 45 minutes before kick-off. One fare only 2d each way". Witton depot's 359 waits for its departure time on 1st October 1938. The white paint on the kerbs are presumably a blackout precaution as the threat of war was imminent at that date.

Below: Another typical Camwell scene to show the setting as well as the tram. This is the Oxhill Road terminus of route 26 at Handsworth with Rookery Road to the right and Stockwell Road on the left. Taken on 7th September 1938, car 601 is ready to return to Colmore Row while 556 and 623 wait their turn to enter the terminal stub.

Above: Under the supervision of the point duty policeman, car 605 turns from Grove Lane into Soho Road on its way from Oxhill Road to City on 7th September 1938. The street layout is still recognizable but the traffic volume has increased a thousandfold.
Below: Holyhead Road, Handsworth, taken from the corner of Station Road looking east. On 30th August 1938, car 517 on a short working to this point on service 28 is about to cross over to return to City. In the centre of the picture is the *New Inns* public house with its prominent "M&B" emblem. The building remains today but has been converted to apartments.

Above: Birmingham's trams ventured outside the City from 1st April 1924 when the Corporation began to work the West Bromwich system on behalf of that authority after expiry of their lease to the South Staffordshire Tramways (Lessee) Company Limited. Through services to Dudley and Wednesbury were established, operated on behalf of the South Staffordshire company beyond West Bromwich. When Birmingham took over, one of the first alterations to be made was the laying of loops to accommodate football specials at The Hawthorns. On 24th September 1938, the same day that Cam recorded the St Andrews specials (see page 16), he went on to The Hawthorns to take this photograph. Although they were in the Second Division that season, the Albion fans should have been happier than the Blues, as West Bromwich beat Tottenham Hotspur 4-3. West Bromwich Corporation decided not to renew the operating agreement when it was due to expire, but to substitute buses. It would have made no sense to split the route at the boundary so, despite being the most profitable group of tram routes in the city, there was little choice but to abandon the Handsworth route and the Wheeler Street and Oxhill Road branches at the same time. Buses duly took over on 2nd April 1939.

Below: 628 and 529 at the Bridge Street, Wednesbury terminus on 13th September 1938. The remains of the curve into Holyhead Road leading to Darlaston and of the line straight on into Lower High Street for Walsall are visible where a Walsall Corporation bus loads for that town.

Above: Birmingham also had a second service to Dudley (see pages 27 to 29). The two routes met at Burnt Tree where, on 6th September 1938, 634 is approaching from West Bromwich and 148 is climbing the hill from Tividale. The "slow" sign and the direction sign beyond mark the Wolverhampton New Road which crossed both routes here in succession, all now replaced by a large roundabout. Behind the cyclist, the narrow gauge rails of a one-time colliery line which crossed the tramway can just be seen in the setts on the original print, the rest of the carriageway having long been re-surfaced.

Below: The terminus of both routes (74 via West Bromwich and 87 via Oldbury) was at the foot of Castle Hill on the railway bridge where, on 9th August 1938, car 518 is disgorging passengers in the background. A late arrival makes a dash as car 523 leaves on the West Bromwich route while 165 will follow it on the Oldbury service. Just visible behind 165 is the side of the Midland Red bus garage, opened in 1929 but now closed and demolished as this whole area now forms a major junction with the start of the Dudley southern bypass.

Above: Still at the Dudley terminus, but now looking in the opposite direction on 13th September 1938, 154 is on service 87 and 596 on the 74. The filled-in tram rails leading up the hill were once the Dudley, Stourbridge & District Electric Traction Company Limited's route between the towns named in its title, closed in 1930. Dudley Hippodrome may be seen approaching completion on the right.

Below: The closure of Hockley depot to trams and the consequent reshuffle of the tramway fleet in April 1939 would lead to the withdrawal of Witton depot's six 71 class cars, hence this picture on 21st September 1938. This was also a fortunate target for the Camwell lens because service 3 to Witton via Six Ways was withdrawn in September 1939 as a wartime economy measure and never resumed. 146 will shortly depart up Witton Road behind the camera and the tram on the 3X service to City via Aston Cross which can just be seen behind 146 will depart along Witton Lane past the depot, now the home of the Aston Manor Road Transport Museum.

Above: Since July 1906, the Dudley Road services had been operated jointly with the Birmingham and Midland Tramways Limited (which changed its name in August 1912 to the Birmingham District Power and Traction Company Limited). In April 1928 the Corporation began to work the section between Grove Lane and Dudley via Oldbury on behalf of the company, so bringing Birmingham trams into Dudley by a second route. The company's route, i.e. outside the Birmingham boundary, was purchased by the various local authorities as from 1st January 1939 so that, from that date, Birmingham was operating on behalf of Smethwick, Oldbury, Rowley Regis, Tipton and Dudley councils. This was purely a temporary arrangement until the trams could be abandoned and a motor bus service, operated jointly by Birmingham and the Midland Red company could be instituted.

Services along the Dudley Road terminated in a loop of streets behind the Birmingham Council House with the loading stands in Edmund Street. On 30th August 1938, car 112 is loading for Spon Lane, Smethwick, on route 85. Ahead of it is 130 bound for Bearwood on route 29 and, below the bridge linking the two parts of the Council House, 256 is on the Lodge Road service 32. Notice the wetness of the rails because here and at other important points a water supply was provided to lubricate curves to reduce noise and also flange wear. The section of track which still remains in pedestrianized Edmund Street has been slightly repositioned from its original alignment.

Opposite lower: Once away from the Dudley Road, Cam seems to have rather neglected the Lodge Road route. No post-war views were taken and we think only this one before the war. Beyond Lodge Road the route continued down Foundry Road to terminate outside the *Railway Inn* on the corner of Wellington Street (seen on the right). Today, the road has become a private one and the public house has also gone. Only the curve of the railway embankment remains to identify this location.

Car 59, photographed on 2nd July 1938, was one of a class of 130 trams, all except seventeen of which had been withdrawn by March 1937. The remaining few were retained for the Lodge Road service as they were the only four-wheel cars with a sufficiently short wheelbase to negotiate safely the sharp bends whilst longer bogie cars, suitable in themselves, would have been unable to pass each other on the corners without a considerable re-positioning of the trackwork. Intended for withdrawal in September 1939, wartime conditions brought a reprieve for route and trams until 29th March 1947. Bow collectors had replaced trolley poles on the Lodge Road service in 1926 and the Washwood Heath routes were similarly converted when new rolling stock came in 1928. There was still talk in 1930 of more conversions but nothing further was done and the low bridges on some routes would have ruled out conversion of the whole system.

Above: This view is taken at the foot of the Parade looking towards the city centre on 27th September 1948. Car 128 heads for Bearwood on service 29, whilst 248 which follows will turn right over the tracks in the foreground up Newhall Hill bound for Winson Green on the Lodge Road 32 service.

Above: Seen crossing Lee Bridge, near the junction of Dudley Road and Heath Street, in August 1939, is 347, one of a pair of 1911 trams which had their top-deck balconies experimentally enclosed in 1921. A number of these 301 class tramcars were cascaded from the Bristol Road services in 1939 where they had been displaced by newer cars. Although the Dudley Road services were converted to bus operation on 1st October 1939, track on this section remained in use until August 1947 so that cars on the Ladywood service could reach Rosebery Street depot. The building on the left is Dudley Road Hospital, now City Hospital and very much rebuilt.
Below: This is Dudley Road at Grove Lane with car 180 about to return to City on 30th August 1938. The conductor, having turned the trolley pole, has stowed the rope through the top pigtail and lower loop and will place the looped rope-end on a hook inside the car. The Grove Cinema across the road still displays its name on high but is now an establishment selling bathrooms and kitchens. Over the years, Birmingham absorbed many of the surrounding local authorities but not Smethwick, with the result that in barely two miles from Edmund Street, the trams had reached the City boundary.

Above: On 30th August 1938, 215 has just reversed in High Street Smethwick, at Cape Hill, to return to Birmingham. In the distance, 190 approaches bound for Spon Lane Smethwick on service 85 whilst behind that can just be seen 190, which will turn left along Waterloo Road to Bearwood on service 29.

Below: Short workings on the Dudley service to Spon Lane were numbered 85 and on 2nd July 1938, 102 has just arrived and will turn back at this point. The direction post in the middle distance marks the actual junction with Spon Lane but nothing of the scene remains today in what is now a wide dual carriageway.

EVENING
DESPATCH
154
QUALITY
MEAT
OLDBURY
PALACE
TO-DAY
WILL
HAY
RIVER

H.C. GRIFFIN
WINE & SPIRIT MERCHANT
86
EVENING DESPATCH
186
CREMALT

Opposite: In Oldbury, the trams encountered the very narrow Birmingham Street which is little changed today. Even a single track in the middle of the road would have meant that another vehicle could not pass a tramcar on either side. Instead, a double line was laid but the tracks had to be positioned so close together that trams could not pass each other. At the end of the narrow street, the tracks converged into an ordinary single line across the Square into Freeth Street so the whole distance had to be worked as one single line section, latterly controlled by signal lights.

In the **upper picture** 154 has just entered Birmingham Street from Oldbury on 23rd August 1939. The use of the Square as a bus terminus is clearly seen in the background with Midland Red and West Bromwich Corporation buses visible.

In the **lower picture** car 186 crosses Oldbury Square on 7th September 1938 on service 86 which was the number used for short-working journeys between Birmingham and Oldbury. When the tram reaches Freeth Street, immediately behind the cameraman, it will reverse for return to Birmingham. The curve of granite setts to the left of the tram leads into Church Street and marks the remains of the track leading to Bromford Lane along which, until 1929, there was a shuttle service to West Bromwich operated by the Birmingham & Midland Tramways Company Ltd. The Midland Red double-decker is on service 217 to Halesowen via Blackheath.

Above: Unusual workings attracted Cam's attention as early as 1939. During the war, blackout restrictions made nightwork on the permanent way very difficult. This is an instance where an alternative route was available which made it possible to carry out the work during the daytime without resort to replacement buses. On various Sundays when the tracks in Digbeth were closed for repairs, the Albert Street tram services were diverted via Bradford Street and Bromsgrove Street to terminate in Hill Street. There had been no regular passenger service over the tracks in Bromsgrove Street and this part of Bradford Street since closure of the Stratford Road routes in January 1937.

On Sunday 5th November 1939, 521 is returning from Hill Street and pauses outside the impressive frontage of the J.B. Machine Tool Company Limited. On the extreme right of this picture can be seen part of the *Anchor* public house which still trades on the corner of Rea Street. 521 will go straight ahead to rejoin its normal route on the far side of the Rea Street junction.

Car 664 leaves Miller Street to take up service on the Erdington service. We are looking north along Elkington Street, with Miller Street to the right.

Miller Street depot was badly damaged by enemy action in the early hours of 10th April 1941. Two high explosive bombs, an oil bomb and several incendiaries hit the office block. Three employees were killed when the Mess Room was hit as the floor of the Social Room fell burying a number of people. The men on duty immediately ran out the hose pipes but unfortunately there was no water. The office block was burnt out together with the top bay of the shed. The 24 trams in the top bay were completely destroyed, although in most cases the trucks and motors were eventually able to be re-used. Other cars were damaged to a greater or lesser extent and over 60 trams in the depot suffered blast damage to their glazing.

Steps were taken to get the fleet back into service as quickly as possible and within a very few days broken glass had been removed and the trams put into service with temporary replacements. In many cases, not all panes were broken but 664 seems to have suffered more than most. Note that in this photo, some of the sheets seem to be flexible whilst other are not, so it would appear that a mixture of board and canvas had to be used. 664 ran in this state for a couple of months, not being called into the works for reglazing until 23rd June.

The photograph also clearly shows the fender painted white to show up in the blackout, the masked headlamp and also the temporary rear lamp (on the right and below the headlamp). Birmingham trams did not have separate rear lamps before the war, the Board of Trade lamp (to the left of the drivers rain shield in this photo) being sufficient but that was too high off the ground to meet wartime lighting regulations. On the right of the picture, the traction standard also carries bands of white paint to assist visibility in the blackout.

Edward Road, Balsall Heath, looking east at the junction with George Street and Tindal Street on 10th June 1941. The *New Moseley Arms* is partially visible behind the tram and is still in business, though it is now *The Clock*. Otherwise, all the property in this view has been cleared and redeveloped. Wartime conditions are clearly visible in the form of white paint on the tramcar fender and platform steps as well as the masked headlamp. Note also the precaution against blast in the form of saloon windows obscured by netting save for a peephole in the centre of each pane; very unpopular with passengers. the practice was soon abandoned. The bollards in the road are also picked out in white as an aid to visibility.

All tram services were badly disrupted after the serious air raid on 9th/10th April 1941. Normal service was resumed on most routes within a matter of weeks but the outward Balsall Heath routes were affected by a large crater in Clevedon Road near Calthorpe Park which had also damaged the gas and water mains. When it became apparent in mid-May that there would be further delay because the Public Works Department needed to repair a damaged sewer, a temporary service, displaying Cannon Hill 37 although it did not reach that district, began on 15th May operating from City via Leopold Street and Moseley Road to reverse outside the Imperial Cinema on the corner of Clifton Road before descending Edward Road to a terminus at the junction with Lincoln Street. The service was then able to return to City via the normal route along Longmore Street and Gooch Street.

As Edward Road was only a depot link, it was unusual for Birmingham in only having a single trolley wire through a passing loop as can be seen in this view. In the unlikely event of cars needing to pass, one of them would have to take its trolley pole off the overhead line. Note also the trolley rope hanging loose, ready for the car to be "trolleyed" round the curve into Lincoln Street.

Even under wartime conditions Cam was there to record unusual features when possible before they disappeared. This is one of his "last day" views as it was the final day of this diversion, the normal service route being resumed from first car the following morning.

The local lads appear to be making the most of the extra mileage for their halfpenny child's tickets.

Originally, the terminus of the Ladywood 33 route was at the Lower Temple Street end of Navigation Street but congestion caused by trams crossing Hill Street to reach the terminus and then back again into John Bright Street led to the service being transferred to the west end of Navigation Street on 23rd November 1929. In any case, where possible Birmingham favoured loop termini in the City Centre to avoid the delay in reversing cars. This group of routes ran in via Suffolk Street and out via John Bright Street and, in common with other loop termini, arriving passengers were decanted from the driver's platform into the carriageway so that the loading and unloading could take place at the same time.

Reprieved from earlier closure by the outbreak of war, the last day of operation was 30th August 1947, when we see 732 **(above)** loading in Navigation Street, followed by an 812 Class car on the Cotteridge service, behind which a good queue has formed for the Bristol Road services to Rednal and Rubery. On the same date, looking north in Icknield Port Road **(below)**, 733 is waiting in the passing loop at Osler Street for 754, seen in the distance at the Wiggin Street loop, to approach.

Further along Icknield Port Road these last day views on 30th August 1947 show car 738 **(above)** entering Gillott Street loop from City. Most of the property at this point has been redeveloped but the shop on the left of the road immediately behind the tram remains as a small independent supermarket and off-licence at the corner of Coplow Street. A minute or so later but looking in the opposite direction, 738 **(below)** is now waiting for 749 to leave the single-track. The road junction just visible on the left marks the corner of Gillott Road. Note the tram stop sign on the right complete with lorry. Inconsiderate parking at public transport stopping places is nothing new. Both cars were from a batch of thirty delivered in 1926, the Corporation's first order for trams equipped with air brakes.

Above: The Bordesley Green routes had been the province of 301 Class cars only since 1939 when they had been displaced from the Bristol Road services allowing older trams (as shown on pages 16 and 17) to be withdrawn. When the Fazeley Street service opened on 24th November 1906, the City terminus had been a loop around Albert Street, High Street, Carrs Lane and Moor Street. In July 1930, the direction of the loop was reversed but to reduce congestion, the terminus was soon curtailed on 5th November 1930 to Albert Street between Moor Street and Seymour Street (about where the lorry may be seen). This photograph, taken on 29th September 1948, shows car 309 waiting at the top of Fazeley Street to which point the terminus had been further curtailed in September 1947. Suspicion of an unexploded bomb brought about that curtailment but services resumed soon afterwards. In November 1947, another scare necessitated further excavations which involved cutting the track on the passing loop. No bomb was found but it was not considered worthwhile to reinstate a line which would soon be abandoned. Buses took over on 3rd October 1948. The building immediately on the photographer's right occupied a triangular site bounded by Albert Street, Fazeley Street and Park Street and is the prominent building furthest away in the lower picture on page 39.

Opposite top: Although the long shadows detract from this picture we think it worth including. On 30th September 1948, car 367 descends Fazeley Street past Bartholomew Street and is about to pass under the railway bridge where car 312 is waiting at the passing loop. The now rebuilt bridge still carries the main railway lines out of New Street to the east but the impressive array of semaphore signals controlled by Proof House Junction has long since given way to colour light signals.

Opposite middle: Looking at the same bridge from the other side, 344 waits under the bridge for 374 to clear the single-line while 386 waits further back to be clear of the junction with New Canal Street on 25th August 1948.

Opposite bottom: At the eastern end of Fazeley Street, the tram route turned left into Great Barr Street where car 336 is seen travelling towards City at Montague Street in another 1948 view. The waste ground on the right is the result of wartime bombing.

BARTHOLOMEW ST
90

MONTAGUE ST
90
EVANS & KITCHEN
Austin

90
313

MAXSTOKE S
EVANS' CIDER

90
GARAGE

Opposite top: On 30th September 1948, car 313 leaves the single track in Great Barr Street and is about to pass 363 waiting in Garrison Lane on the other side of Lawley Street. This busy junction later became traffic-light controlled and is now the site of a large roundabout. The tram standard has not been repainted since the end of the war as it still carries the white paint blackout guidance markings. The view shows to advantage the bracket arm supporting the overhead wires, usual in Birmingham on single track as opposed to the more common span-wire construction with standards either side of the road on double track. Note on the left, the bus stop post erected in readiness for the changeover. After the last car on Saturday night, the tram stops would be removed and the flags added to the new bus stop posts before the Sunday service began.

Opposite middle: Descending Garrison Lane towards City, 357 negotiates the short single line section over the narrow canal bridge on 25th August 1948. This section is now much wider but the junction with Maxstoke Street will help to identify it.

Opposite lower: On 29th September 1948, tram 350 is entering Garrison Lane from Bordesley Green bound for City. The tracks in the foreground lead into Cattell Road which was traversed by an alternative service 84 between City and Stechford via Deritend. The second tram is 315 bound for Coventry Road depot and will take the Cattell Road line to reach its destination.

This junction was always known as "The Atlas" from the public house of that name which occupied the fork of Cattell Rd and Garrison Lane. The road layout at this point is basically unchanged but only the angle of the junction provides a link with the past as none of the property shown now exists.

Above: Moving further from the city, Cam is now at Belchers Lane where Bordesley Green becomes Bordesley Green East and the trams passed through the roundabout and onto a central reservation on the dual carriageway. The second carriageway was not constructed for some time after the service began so the trams were effectively running on a roadside reservation during that period. Known as the Broadway junction this is still a recognizable scene though the *Broadway* pub off camera to the left no longer fulfils that role and is currently a McDonalds.

On 29th September 1948, car 365 is inbound from Stechford on service 90 with 326 on service 84 coming up the hill behind it.

At the top of Kingston Hill, Coventry Road curves to the right whilst Cattell Road leads straight on towards Bordesley Green. On 29th September 1948, car 368 **(above)** bound for Stechford waits while 314 clears the single track in Cattell Road. A minute or so later, **(below)** 314 in turn waits to give priority to 326 coming out of the depot to take up service on the same route. The depot was shared by trams and trolleybuses as the overhead wiring clearly demonstrates and was officially known as Arthur Street but was frequently referred to as Coventry Road. When it became a bus garage, Coventry Road was adopted as the official name

Above: On 11th July 1949, 445 has unloaded at the top of Carrs Lane, to run empty along High Street and turn into Albert Street to reach the loading point for service 42 to Alcester Lanes End. Looking straight ahead is Dale End where, in the middle distance car 770 has arrived from Washwood Heath and will turn right to its terminus in Martineau Street. The overhead wiring of the connecting link between the two routes appears clearly; note the insulated crossing where the wire for the connecting line crossed the trolleybus negative wire.

Below: The track was moved to the kerbside in Albert Street after the direction of the terminal loop was reversed in 1930. At the same time the glazed-roof shelters were constructed by the Corporation, which paid one shilling a year acknowledgment to the leaseholder for the right to erect them and attach them to the buildings. On 28th June 1949, once the timekeeper has authorized departure, 436 will turn into Moor Street (in front of the building with the white lettering which reads W. Little & Sons Ltd)

Above: From its City terminus, the 42 service ran along Moor Street where 413 is seen topping the rise on the last day of the route's operation on 1st October 1949. This view is quite unrecognizable today as everything was swept away for the Inner Ring Road scheme; only Moor Street Queensway and Moor Street railway station remain to perpetuate the name. The inbound tram track may be seen curving into Carrs Lane to form the terminal loop via High Street to Albert Street.

Opposite: The dualling of Digbeth has transformed this scene although many of the buildings on the left still exist at the time of writing including the erstwhile Digbeth Institute, now the Digbeth Civic Hall. On the left, the *Bull's Head* public house is still open but the impressive building of H. Goodman and Sons now forms part of South Birmingham College and all the buildings on the right have been redeveloped.

Trolleybus 74 **(upper)** on peak-period service 93 turns from High Street Deritend into Rea Street on its way to Station Street on 28th June 1949. The only trackwork in use is the curve in the foreground, the remainder having been out of use since the Stechford abandonment the previous October. A minute or two later and only a yard or two away, we see 416 **(lower)** in Digbeth, about to turn right into Rea Street. Service 50 was a short working on the Alcester Lanes End service as far as Trafalgar Road but was chiefly used for workings running in to Moseley Road depot at that point. The "depot only" destination was not used from City to this depot as Birmingham was very careful to avoid confusion at central termini. From Albert Street, "depot only" was only used on trams bound for Arthur Street depot whilst, until 1937, 45 had similarly distinguished trams to Highgate Road depot.

The overhead wiring is prominent, highlighting another of Cam's specialities. When developing his own negatives by hand he often under-exposed the sky areas in order to bring out overhead detail without detracting from the other parts of the photograph.

There was no separate tram and trolleybus wiring between Albert Street and Rea Street and the trams simply used the trolleybus positive wire. 416 has just passed under the automatic point turner in the overhead which was actuated by the driver applying power for one direction and not doing so for the other. At this particular junction it was just possible for a trolleybus following too closely to derail a tram by changing the points beneath it; it happened at least once.

H. GOODMAN
& SONS
NAMEPLATES
YARDLEY AND
STATION STREET 93
COX 74

50
CAVES
DEWARS
everybody's

Opposite top: This is Hill Street terminus, showing Birmingham's unique short section of triple track. Car 442 on the Trafalgar Road via Leopold Street service will shortly turn right to terminate at the point shown in the photograph below and on return will use the centre track at this point.

In this 22nd June 1949 photograph, 716 is on the Cannon Hill service and car 441 behind is bound for Alcester Lanes End via Balsall Heath on service 39. These trams will have crossed from the inbound line on a crossover just behind the photographer and on departure will continue along the third track.

When the Coventry Road trams were abandoned in January 1934, the Station Street terminus was taken out of use and the Stratford Road services which also used that point were diverted to Hill Street where they had to turn with the Balsall Heath cars and then return to a new loading point on the third track just to the right of this photograph. This caused considerable congestion at the Hill Street terminus and even when the Stratford Road services ended in January 1937 there were still complaints from the police because when two trams were in the terminus at once, the further one was standing across a pedestrian crossing as in this view.

Below: Round the corner from Hill Street was the Navigation Street terminus where car 446 is waiting time to depart to Kings Heath via Leopold Street in Summer 1949. Further back a bus stands at the Midland Red loading point on service 125 to Wolverhampton. The destination blind shows Astwood Bank but close inspection will reveal that conductor has been recorded in the midst of changing the blind.

The tram is standing opposite the foot of Pinfold Street where the Navigation Street entrance to New Street railway station is in 2007. The tall building behind the tram is the back of the Queens Hotel which was demolished with the rebuilding of the station in the 1960s.

On the footpath is the Bundy time recording clock. These were a common sight at most Birmingham bus or tram termini. They were introduced in the very early years of the system and lasted well into West Midlands PTE days. Each driver carried a key with a unique number and was required to register with the Bundy clock whereon his key impression was stamped on a roll of paper alongside the time. The time was checked and the rolls changed by a designated inspector each morning and were subsequently scrutinized at the depots for any irregularities.

Below: This photograph was taken on 1st October 1949, last day of operation of the Moseley tramway services. Car 431 is in Hill Street, at the point where the third track joins the ordinary outward line shortly before the junction with Station Street, and will run to Trafalgar Road via Leopold Street. Only just visible in the right background is car 429 on service 39 at the Hill Street terminus shown in the upper picture.

Bus 1679 at the stop opposite is a Brush-bodied Leyland which has come from Warstock on service 24 whilst behind the tram can be seen one of Hockley garage's Leyland-bodied Leylands on service 16A from Yardley to Hamstead.

The "Futurist Theatre" sign marks the back of what by then was a cinema whose front entrance was in John Bright Street.

At the south end of Rea Street, on 28th June 1949, 446 **(above)** turns from Bradford Street on its way from Alcester Lanes End to Albert Street. 429 is following on service 48, the short-working between City and Kings Heath Church only and is trailed by a wartime Guy utility bus probably from Yardley Wood heading for town but displaying the destination "Ethel Street" because it will turn short at that point rather than completing the usual City Centre loop via Corporation Street and Colmore Row. The tyre agency looks rather as though it may have shut up shop. Today the building has been replaced and of course there is no longer a police telephone. While 446 went into town and returned, Cam has walked to the top of Bradford Street where 446 on its return trip **(below)** turns right into Moseley Road. The tracks straight ahead lead to Camp Hill where Holy Trinity Church can be seen in the background. Although the Stratford Road tramway services had closed in January, 1937, it was necessary to retain the route as far as Kyotts Lake Road as that was the location of the tramcar overhaul works.

In addition to the lines via Bradford Street or via Balsall Heath, there was a third tram route to Moseley. Leaving the Balsall Heath route at the foot of Hurst Street, it ran via Macdonald Street, Thomas Street and Leopold Street to join Moseley Road. In post-war years, this service normally ran only to Trafalgar Road as service 41 but in the rush hours journeys ran through to Kings Heath as service 40.

In the picture **(above)**, 431 has just crossed Dymoke Street on 1st October 1949 and is about to tackle the steeply graded section of Leopold Street; magazine and newspaper wholesalers, Smiths News Plc now occupy the site of the corner shop. On 28th June 1949, **(below)** 408 has reached the top of Leopold Street and turns into Moseley Road where in the distance Brush bodied Leyland 1660 is working the Maypole service.

Above: Included in Cam's summer 1949 survey of the Moseley tram services was a record of bus service 35 to the Maypole. This was a minimum fare service because it paralleled the tram service as far as Alcester Lanes End. The route was to be withdrawn with the Moseley Road trams because the replacement services were to be extended to the Maypole. This picture was taken at the city terminus in Station Street near the back entrance to New Street railway station. Although the station has been transformed, the roadway is still in the same place.

Bus 1161 is a 1939 Daimler but in April 1949 it had been re-bodied with this distinctive English Electric body, one of a number built for Manchester Corporation in 1940 which never entered service there as the chassis for which they were intended were destroyed by enemy action at the Daimler factory in Coventry. In 1942, Birmingham purchased twenty of these bodies to replace some of their own losses by enemy action. By 1949 some bodies which had been mounted on older chassis due for withdrawal were then transferred to newer vehicles as seen here.

Trolleybus 81 is about to overtake to reach its own loading point on the peak hour service 93 to Yardley.

Opposite: These three pictures, all taken on 22nd June 1949, illustrate the services threading the Balsall Heath area. The street pattern remains in most cases but the area has been completely redeveloped. Because of the narrow roads, the Balsall Heath and Cannon Hill routes were laid along separate roads outwards and inwards. This mode of operation occurred in various places around the world and became known to tramway enthusiasts as "Cannon Hilling". 728 **(above)** turns from Gooch Street into Sherlock Street on its way to Hill Street; nothing remains today except the road layout. A little further out, **(middle)** 725 has just turned from Sherlock Street into St Luke's Road where the only building to remain today is the distant school on the curve (now the Highgate Centre of Birmingham Social Services). Finally **(below)** 441 turns from Alexandra Road into Balsall Heath Road outward bound to Kings Heath in yet another picture where absolutely no buildings remain from the era illustrated. Another "Camwellism" well illustrated in the lower two views, was his care to ensure that street names were included where possible to avoid any doubts about the location.

TyPhoo TEA
EVENING DESPAT
728

SHERLOCK St
COGSWELL

38
BOVRIL
PUTS BEEF INTO YOU
BALSALL HEATH Rd

Above: Here tram 721, travelling towards City in Mary Street, is about to turn into the short Balfour Street before turning right into Lincoln Street on 27th June 1949. Again, everything has been redeveloped but the road grid and names have been retained.

Below: At the south end of Court Road the outward routes diverged. The curve in the foreground carried (from left to right) the outward Cannon Hill service into Cannon Hill Road, whilst cars to Alcester Lanes End turned left behind the tram illustrated and climbed Edward Road as far as Mary Street. Only workings from depot used the third side of the triangle. On 27th June 1949, 719 has come down Edward Road from the depot and run against the flow of outward tram traffic from Mary Street in order to take up service at Cannon Hill. Surprisingly, the row of shops and the solitary private house are much the same in 2007 even down to the enamelled road sign over the shop.

Above: The Cannon Hill service was unusual in not starting up on weekdays until 7.30am. When Moseley Road depot was being converted to accommodate buses, the number of cars which could be housed overnight was reduced so it was therefore convenient for a number of cars to be parked out overnight in Cannon Hill Road and run directly into service the next morning. This picture taken at 7.0am on 6th July 1949, shows 424 about to depart; in due course the supervising inspector will despatch 427, 433, 728, 417, 722, 412, 729 and 731.
Below: At the south end of Cannon Hill Road the 37 service turned into Edgbaston Road and left again into Willows Road to return to City. On 27th June 1949, 728 turns into the main road opposite Cannon Hill Park main gate in a scene easily recognizable today.

Above: Showing how much the trams had to "cut the corner" to cope with the narrow streets in the Balsall Heath area, car 448 running from City to Alcester Lanes End is turning from Edward Road into Mary Street on 27th June 1949. Apart from the property immmediately on the right and the side of the *Coach and Horses* public house across Mary Street, everything else visible has been cleared and redeveloped.

Below: Apart from a short-lived service in 1907, the top part of Edward Road east of Mary Street carried only Moseley Road depot cars taking up or finishing service. At the start of the evening rush hour on 27th June 1949, car 389 has come from depot, reversed at the top of Edward Road and is beginning the turn right into Mary Street to take up the normal 39 service route to City.

Above: Still at the same junction as the two pictures opposite, we are looking up Mary Street from Edward Road. 366 has just negotiated the curve outbound to resume normal double line running. 440 will continue straight along Mary Street before turning into Balfour Street. This photograph was taken on 1st October 1949, the last day of tramcar operation from Moseley depot.

Below: A typical scene outside Moseley Road depot on 28th June 1949. When the depot was opened in 1907, much publicity was given to its having been constructed to a higher architectural standard than the other new depots built at that time because it was in a residential area. In this view car 427 from Albert Street will work to Kings Heath Church but is having to wait for 435 on service 41 to cross over and start its return journey to City via Leopold Street. Approaching from the Moseley direction are 418 and 407 both on service 42 from Alcester Lanes End to Albert Street.

Above: Short working journeys between City and Balsall Heath turned on a crossover at the top of Mary Street just before Edgbaston Road. Until 1911, this was the City boundary and alternate cars terminated here but the number of short journeys was gradually reduced with more development further out. By 1949 there remained only two morning peak journeys. On 6th July, the 7.26am from Hill Street has reversed its trolley pole and is about to cross over to start its return journey. There is still a shop on the corner of George Street as seen here.
Below: After crossing Edgbaston Road the route continued up Park Road to join Moseley Road. Photographed almost at the junction with Edgbaston Road, 406 follows 328 up the hill towards Moseley Village on 1st October 1949, the last day of service. The replacement buses ran via Willows Road and Salisbury Road and there has never been a public transport service along Mary Street or Park Road since.

Most of the property in this **(upper)** view at Moseley Village on 29th June 1949 is superficially unchanged although the Birmingham Municipal Bank is now a "Select and Save" minimarket. 409 on the Leopold Street service carries the traditional livery being last repainted in April 1946. Later that year a simplified style without cream rocker panels or lining-out came into use; this was further modified in October 1948 by the substitution of fleet numbers with unshaded numerals. 405, on the service from Albert Street, was only repainted in February 1949 even though it was known that it would be scrapped in October the same year, an indication of the high standards which Birmingham tried to maintain. Both cars will turn at High Street, Kings Heath, opposite All Saints Church, recorded **(below)** on the same day. Only in the rush hour would two trams be reversing together at this point, 426 on 48 to Albert Street and 728 on 38 to Hill Street. Note the convenience of a third overhead wire for the poles of cars reversing here.

Above: Before the Walsall Road at Great Barr near the *Scott Arms* was made into a dual carriageway, there was a service road on the east side between Queslett Road and Calshot Road which was used by buses from Walsall to Birmingham and as a layover point for buses from Birmingham turning round at this point where our picture was taken.

Until 1928, this area formed part of Perry Barr Urban District and was therefore Midland Red "territory". When Perry Barr was absorbed into Birmingham, the Midland Red Walsall service became one which was operated on behalf of Birmingham within the City boundary. As housing developments took place in the 1930s, regular short workings were added between City and Scott Arms and a branch service to Beeches Estate introduced.

On 16th July 1949, there was a Midland Film and Theatrical Garden Fête at the Chateau Impney, Droitwich. All proceeds were in aid of Press Charities and Honor Blackman, Petula Clark, Diana Dors, Donald Houston and Bill Owen were among those billed to appear. The Midland Red company required many extra vehicles for their service 144 to work between Birmingham and Droitwich and so it was arranged that the Corporation would take over most, if not all, of the workings on the Great Barr and Beeches Estate services just for the day.

Unfortunately, the weather didn't look too promising when this Midland Red wartime Daimler from Digbeth garage passed on its way from Walsall as the Corporation's Daimler drafted in from Liverpool Street garage waits departure time on the Great Barr service.

When the required wording was not on a destination blind, it was the practice in Birmingham to use a board across the radiator, as seen here. The introduction of buses with concealed radiators meant that this useful custom had to go but, to alleviate the difficulty to some extent, suffix letters were gradually allocated to the route numbers to identify regular short-working destinations.

By chance, the Corporation bus photographed was 1822 which, after only a fortnight in service, had been lent to the Board of Trade along with two Birmingham crews from 30th August to 12th October 1948 in connection with the British Exhibition in Copenhagen. The outward and return route was overland (with ferry crossings of course) through Belgium, Holland and Germany. Six vehicles from different operators (not all Daimlers) were in the convoy. During the actual exhibition from 18th September to 3rd October, the vehicles operated a passenger service in Copenhagen linking the various buildings of the exhibition. After its return, a plate was affixed to the lower saloon bulkhead of 1822 recording its exploit.

Martineau Street was the city terminus for some of the northern routes. Trams ran in via Dale End to Martineau Street leaving via Corporation Street. Martineau Street no longer exists, being redeveloped during the 1960s. Furthest away from the camera **(above)** 726 is just turning into Corporation Street in front of the Cobden Hotel which stood on the corner of Cherry Street where Rackhams (now House of Fraser) store is. Behind it is car 632 on the Perry Barr service, which loaded at the top stand in Martineau Street, with 725 following. 725 and 726 are not in service as they are in course of transfer from Moseley Road depot to Miller Street depot for further service on 1st October 1949. Earlier in the year **(below)** and looking in the opposite direction from Corporation Street, car 20 loads for Perry Barr, with what is probably 576 on the same service waiting to load; lower down 769 on service 10 to Washwood Heath leads three more trams waiting their turn.

In 2007, only the Central Fire Station building remains to identify this spot. The junction was originally called Central Place but was renamed Corporation Place on 9th July 1936. On 23rd September 1943 it was further renamed to Lancaster Place and later to Lancaster Circus.

Car 666 on the Erdington 2 service **(upper)** approaches Steelhouse Lane as 585 passes outbound. 666 had been followed by open balcony car 400 on service 3X from Witton which is turning out of Aston Street into Stafford Street making for Martineau Street. Next comes 650 on service 79 from Pype Hayes which was so close behind 400 that it is already crossing the points which 400 has barely cleared. Minutes later, **(lower)** it is the turn of the Perry Barr service: car 17 joins the Steelhouse Lane tracks from Corporation Street and will immediately turn left into Lancaster Street while in the background, car 18 crosses out of Lancaster Street into Stafford Street.

An unusual Alvis with van body (JYF 52) is parked on the right and our lower picture happens to have captured the approach of HNP 535, a brand new Sentinel lorry of E.P. Hingley Ltd (they were fruit and potato merchants, from Blackheath).

Above: This shot shows Car 3 at the top of Lancaster Street heading towards the City on 12th July 1949. This area has changed beyond recognition with Lancaster Circus and its flyover now dominating the view. On the left of the picture is the warehouse of Halfords Cycle Co. Ltd which was destroyed by fire on 12th March 1955 and the site, subsequently used for the West Midlands County Council offices, is now occupied by Birmingham City Council. Beyond it may be seen the end of the Central Fire Station building, about the only bricks and mortar still surviving from the time of the photo.
Below: On 6th July 1949, 668 is just starting away from the compulsory stop at Lower Tower Street in New Town Row outward from City with car 8 is close behind. This is now a wide dual-carriageway and only the names of the roads remain to locate this scene.

Perry Barr was Cam's local route so it is not surprising that he documented it fairly thoroughly before its demise on 31st December 1949. The coverage is especially useful as this is probably the route where road developments have most transformed the townscape. These two views on 6th July 1949 show **(above)** car 18 in New Town Row at the junction with Miller Street looking south with the tracks to the depot of that name leading off on the left and **(below)** New Town Row becomes High Street Aston and we are looking north this time as car 451 approaches on the interlaced track between Webster Street and Phillips Street. Yet another view where everything in the picture has gone but, in the background, notice the Aston Hippodrome music hall. The Drum, a contemporary arts centre now occupies the site of the music hall and will help to locate the view.

Above: Looking north this time, the Trinity Road flyover now stands where the tram is city-bound from Perry Barr in Birchfield Road at New Inn Road on 5th July 1949. The spire of Holy Trinity Church above the tram remains to pinpoint the spot. Car 710, only six months out of the paint shop and without any external advertisements, shows off the final version of Birmingham's tramcar livery to advantage.

Below: Also on 5th July 1949, tram 662 is further along Birchfield Road. The road leading off on the right is Thornbury Road and the Odeon picture house (currently the Royale Suite) was immediately on the photographer's right. The distinguished building on the next corner was a branch of the Birmingham Municipal Bank; still performing a similar function it is now a branch of Lloyds TSB.

Above: This view is looking towards City in High Street Aston. All the buildings have now been cleared but the location can be identified by reference to the still extant *Bartons Arms* public house which is just behind the photographer on the opposite side of the road. Visible on the original print is the wording "Bartons Arms", one of the few names to appear in the "number" box at each end of the tramcar. The shadows are long but evening was the only time that cars could be photographed using this crossover when extras ran a shuttle service between this point and Perry Barr on the occasion of greyhound or speedway racing at the two stadia near the terminus. On 11th July 1949, car 692 prepares to return to Perry Barr.

Above: Birchfield Road looking north at the corner of Bragg Road. The Birchfield cinema, closed in March 1962, is prominent; that corner site is now occupied by the Pak Supermarket though set back slightly more from the road, while the Perry Barr underpass has absorbed everything to the left.

On Monday 11th July 1949, 692 approaches followed by 317, both displaying "Depot Only" as they are running to Miller Street depot. 396 is standing almost outside the entrance to Birchfield Road bus garage and, followed by 452, waits to go forward into the terminus at Perry Barr Station. Trams waiting to enter the terminus had to stand this far back, well clear of the traffic lights at Wellington Road junction, in the slightly wider section of road where vehicles could pass between tram and kerb.

301 Class cars (as represented by 317 and 396) were not scheduled on the Perry Barr route, but this is a speedway racing night and the extra services were usually covered by voluntary overtime at the end of normal duties. It was customary for some of the evening peak services on the Aston Road routes worked by the 301 class to return to Miller Street and immediately continue on to the Perry Barr route.

Opposite: The Perry Barr route encountered a short stretch of single track in Birchfield Road between Mansfield Road and Chain Walk, the junction with the latter is immediately on the right in this view. All the property on the left has now been cleared and widening in connection with the Six Ways underpass has removed everything on the right. This point was the boundary between Aston Manor and Handsworth until both districts were absorbed into Birmingham in 1911. Disagreements over through running meant that for a couple of years passengers had to change from one car to another at this point and during that period a spare tram was usually positioned on the single line to act as a waiting room.

Trams 18 and 3 seen approaching on 5th July 1949 are from the first order of twenty trams to be built for Birmingham Corporation. Originally open-topped they were top covered in two batches in 1905 and 1907. Although imposing to look at, their 16ft 8in height restricted their sphere of operation as they could not pass under any of the low bridges (Aston, Selly Oak and later Dudley Port) on the system. Consequently they spent most of their lives on the Perry Barr route which they largely monopolized until twelve of their number were lost in the Miller Street depot air raid. As two others had already been withdrawn, this left just six to soldier on until withdrawal in 1949 with 45 years service to their credit.

Two more views where all the buildings pictured have gone. Immediately behind car 400 **(above)** is the cross roads of Aston Road with Bracebridge Street to the left and Dartmouth Street on the right, all now completely lost under Dartmouth Circus. On 31st December 1949, last day of operation of the Witton service, 773 from Washwood Heath depot works a football special for Villa Park and 400 is on an extra 3X working for the same reason. The other picture **(below)** is taken in Aston Road North at Avenue Road with St Mary's Church on the corner of Avenue Road to the right and the bulk of Ansell's Brewery just visible in the far distance. Car 690 is bound for Erdington on service 2 whilst 395 is running from Witton to City. 395 is the only Birmingham tram still to exist and is now housed at Thinktank, Birmingham's Science Museum at Millenium Point.

Two more Saturday views in 1949, thought to be taken on 31st December. 375 **(above)** in Park Road is approaching Aston Cross from Witton, while a good crowd of football supporters wait for a tram in the opposite direction. This section of Park Road was later closed off and taken over by Ansells Brewery but since the brewery was closed and demolished, Park Road has reappeared on its original alignment as a cul-de-sac to industrial premises.

Looking down Park Road, Aston **(below)** 635 heads for Witton on service 3X, while Miller Street's 660, showing Football Special on the blind, returns to town for another load. Aston Church identifies the location but most of this section of Park Road is now covered by the Aston Expressway and what remained has been thrown back into Aston Park on the left.

We couldn't show football extras at St Andrews and The Hawthorns and omit Villa Park! On 10th September 1949, Aston Villa were at home to Blackpool (it was a goalless draw) and the football extras are on hand to take the crowds home. At this time, regular attendances of over 40,000 could be expected for first class matches and the impressive organization to clear the crowds promptly at the end of the match had to be seen to be believed. Within thirty minutes of the final whistle, it was all over and everyone had gone.

In Trinity Road **(above)**, the extras stood for the duration of the match as this loop around Trinity Road and Bevington Road had not been part of a service route for nearly forty years before this photograph was taken. The crew of the third tram along are sitting on the platform step, an indication of the sparseness of other road traffic. For the record the cars are 301, 386, 811, 389, 788, 766, 790 and 795.

On the other side of the ground, Witton Lane had to be kept clear for the 3X service to operate and football extras standing in Bevington Road or stabled in Witton depot were moved into position shortly before the end of play. Looking from near the Holte Hotel, **(opposite top)** 642, 359, 396, 361, 677, 380 and 573 await their passengers.

The overhead wiring between City and Witton was made suitable for bow-collector equipped trams specifically so that Washwood Heath depot could provide football extras but they could not operate into Witton depot. Therefore, the usual post-war operation was for Trinity Road and Bevington Road to hold cars from Moseley Road and Washwood Heath (and previously Arthur Street) whilst the Miller Street cars went into the depot.

Villa Park has expanded on both sides since these views were taken. The houses in Witton Lane were demolished and the road moved a few yards to take their place so that the new stand could be built. The kink in Witton Lane near the Trinity Road junction gives the game away. More recently, the new Trinity Road stand has bridged over the road of that name so that the trams furthest away in our view would now be under cover of the new building.

Below: In this evening rush hour view of Aston Cross on 8th August 1949, 385 has just terminated. The conductress has almost completed turning the trolleypole to put it onto the from-city wire, ready for the car to cross over and load up; 660 travelling from Erdington to City waits for its path to be cleared. It was the custom on the Aston Road routes to display the appropriate front number and nearside destination but leave the offside and rear showing the return service when operating short workings such as this, hence the display of 60 on the rear of 385 but Short Heath 78 in the side destination box. The tracks and wiring in the foreground are the Park Road line leading to Witton. The clock tower has since been removed to a different position nearby but the one-time Barclays Bank building on the right remains in 2007 to identify the setting.

Above: In an area completely re-developed twice over since this picture was taken in 1949, 804 has just reached the foot of James Watt Street on the Washwood Heath route as a 637 class car travelling from Perry Barr to City on route 6 is crossing from Stafford Street to join the inward Washwood Heath route in Dale End. As James' Stores advertises, the road ahead is Coleshill Street where normal double line working was resumed at the end of the city terminal loop.

Below: A few yards away from the previous picture, the photographer is standing on the corner of Dale End and James Watt Street, looking into Coleshill Street where cars 775 and 767 are passing on the Washwood Heath service on 12th July 1949. On the corner of Stafford Street, the Corner Café later became the Shah Jahan, one of Birmingham's first Indian restaurants; now all is lost beneath James Watt Queensway.

Above: This the south end of Great Francis Street and the *Junction* public house on the left is in the fork with Bloomsbury Street. 344 from Washwood Heath and 774 from Alum Rock are inbound to City and are about to curve right into Ashted Row. Although most of the Saltley services were operated by trams equipped with bow collectors, there were usually a few cars with trolley poles at Washwood Heath depot where they were confined to low mileage turns. Today Bloomsbury Street and Ashted Row no longer exist and the buildings on the right have also vanished.

Below: Only the gas holders of Saltley Gas Works dominating the background remain to place this view today. This is the foot of Great Francis Street (the remains of which are now Little Hall Road) with Saltley Road, crossing in the background. Tram 791 on its way from Washwood Heath to Martineau Street has to wait for 806 which has arrived on a peak hour short working and will cross over to return to the outer terminus.

Above: Washwood Heath Road, Ward End, looking from City; Sladefield Road leads off on the right immediately behind the prominent lighting standard. This was the original terminus of the Washwood Heath route from 1907. In 1913, the route was extended to the *Fox and Goose* at Bromford Lane and the original terminus then saw only peak-hour short workings which were later allotted service number 9. In this picture 792 is about to return to City

Washwood Heath itself is the high ground in the area where Washwood Heath depot was built and in usual Birmingham style, the tram route carried the same name even though it continued to Ward End. When the service was extended to the *Fox and Goose* in 1913, it was still known as the Washwood Heath route and the district around the newer terminus sometimes became known as Washwood Heath which is not really the case. Unlike the Corporation, the Midland Red company was always careful to define the *Fox and Goose* as being at Ward End in their timetables.

Below: In order to free space in Washwood Heath depot during its conversion for motor buses, tramcars were stabled from 1st January 1950 on the reserved track section of Washwood Heath Road between Twyford Road and the Alum Rock Road. A temporary crossover was installed near Twyford Road and cars turned back here outside the peak periods. In this view, looking west from the junction of Alum Rock Road, cars 764 and 811 are at the head of the line.

Above: In this 1950 view in the yard alongside Washwood Heath depot, wartime Daimler utility 1365 with Duple bodywork was probably photographed as that type of vehicle was being withdrawn and would be all gone by the end of the year. Unlike many operators who rebuilt the utility bodywork for further service, Birmingham's view was that this was not worthwhile in view of the deficiencies of the chassis compared with their usual standards. The destination displayed is a "Camwellism" and unlikely to be the imminent destination of the vehicle. 1365 was withdrawn on 30th November 1950.

Below: A Lichfield City to Birmingham New Street local service calls at Chester Road station in 1950. The three coach train is hauled by 42604, one of a batch constructed by the North British Locomotive Company in 1936 for the London Midland & Scottish Railway Company. We have no idea what prompted this picture, which does not seem to be part of a series. The station is still open but the wooden buildings have long since gone.

Above: The Coventry Road trolleybuses were to be withdrawn at the end of June 1951. At Bordesley Station trolleybus 55 inbound to City on service 99 passes Crossley motor bus 2423, only placed in service on 1st June 1950. The overhead wires under the bridge were supported from troughing attached to the steelwork and, as was customary, a rental was paid to the railway for the privilege. Note the worst irregularities of the abandoned Stechford tram tracks have been patched with tar.

Below: At Wagon Lane turning point trolleybus 62 on a 99 service waits to turn into New Coventry Road from Coventry Road as 33 passes on its way from Lode Lane to City. This turning point had been authorized as part of the original Sheldon extension in 1936 but was only constructed and brought into use from 24th January 1949 when a number of evening peak workings were introduced to reduce unnecessary mileage incurred by running the whole service through to Arden Oak Road.

Above: In 1951, trolleybus 71 leaves Arthur Street (Coventry Road) depot for City to take up service while 59 waits and Crossley 2281 from Liverpool Street garage on the 15B service hastens past, in a similar scenario to that recorded on page 38. The depot building still stands, now occupied by an entertainment technology company.

Below: Trolleybus 32 and another are at Hay Mills looking from City with the *Plough and Harrow* public house beyond the two vehicles. In tramway days, a number of journeys turned on a crossover at this point but with the advent of trolleybuses it was necessary to construct a special turning circle, clearly shown by the overhead wiring in this view. The land formed part of Hay Barn Recreation Ground and the Tramways and Omnibus Department had to lease a plot of land from the Parks Department for the purpose. By the time of this 1951 view only a few morning and midday peak journeys were booked to turn at this point.

The Rover Works was one of the "shadow factories" constructed for the government and operated by the Rover Car company for the construction of aircraft and tank engines. A branch trolleybus route nearly one and a half miles long was constructed under wartime emergency powers to serve the works and brought into use on 29th October 1941. It diverged from the Coventry Road at the *Wheatsheaf* and ran along Lode Lane and Hobs Moat Road, turning down the private road, later Valiant Way, to terminate at the works main entrance. The cost was met by the Ministry of Aircraft Production and revenue from fares on that section, less the Corporation's operating costs, accrued to the Ministry. Service 96 ran from Albert Street whilst 97 was allocated to, but never used for, a possible Station Street service. At the Wheatsheaf junction **(above)**, 79 waits to emerge from Lode Lane and follow 54 towards the City. At the Rover Works **(below)**, trolleybus 20 is the first of four awaiting the onrush of workers.

The Sheldon terminus at the junction of Coventry Road with Arden Oak Road with **(above)** two of the original batch of 50 six-wheeled Leyland buses. The first bus, displaying "Depot Only", is off to Coventry Road depot, whilst the second awaits departure time. The picture has been framed to record the whole of the turning circle in its setting. In the background a Midland Red D5 is loading for Coventry.

A disconnected line of wiring continued from Arden Oak Road to a section feeder situated some distance beyond the terminus. This was because the route was authorized to run as far as the city boundary some 700 yards further on in the expectation of further housing development. The subsequent construction of Elmdon airport ensured that there would be no such development so Arden Oak Road always remained the furthest east for Birmingham trolleybuses. In this view **(lower)** across the road from the previous one, the feeder wiring can just be seen.

Football excursions from Stourbridge to Witton for Villa Park ran via Smethwick Junction, Galton Junction, Handsworth Wood and Perry Barr but continuing pre-nationalization practice, changed from a Western Region engine to a London Midland one at Galton Junction. Under British Railways, it was eventually arranged for the Western Region locomotive to work through. The first occasion this happened was when Aston Villa met Derby County on 25th August 1951 and 9450 **(above)**, only two months old, was photographed joining the Wolverhampton-Birmingham main line at Galton Junction, Smethwick. Sometime in the following season, Cam photographed one of the return workings from Witton. 9477 **(below)** has just emerged from Hamstead Tunnel and is passing through the site of Handsworth Wood station closed to passengers on 5th May 1941. The course of the ramps from road to platforms can just be made out. The road in the background is Hamstead Road and the Birmingham Corporation bus would be on the 15A service from Hamstead to Yardley. The large building immediately above the tunnel mouth is the Endwood Hotel.

Birmingham's longest and best remembered tram route was along the Bristol Road to the Lickey Hills at Rednal. The City terminus was a loop of tracks using Suffolk Street, Navigation Street and John Bright Street. In these 1952 views, we see the inward and outward routes meeting at Horse Fair **(above)** with cars 802 and 811 on the Rubery service 71. Changed beyond recognition with only a few of the buildings on the left of Suffolk Street remaining for identification, this area is now Holloway Circus Queensway; on the right, this end of John Bright Street has been built across so that we can no longer look along the street to note the Council House clock ("Big Brum") on the skyline. A few yards further from city, 733 **(below)** on the Rednal 70 service is just passing the junction with Essex Street.

The Bristol Road services passed onto a central reservation where the dual carriageway began shortly after Priory Road and these pictures are at the junction with Pebble Mill Road where the Cotteridge service branched off. The trees have been allowed to flourish with little pruning for many years but the scene is still fairly easy to recognize today as the distinctive building on the corner of Pebble Mill Road remains; a children's home when photographed, it is now occupied by Aquarius, an alcohol and drugs addiction charity. The two Bundy clocks provided for drivers in either direction to register without leaving their platform can be seen between the tracks just beyond the crossover line. 810 from Rubery **(above)** waits to allow a Cotteridge service to precede it and **(below)** car 519 bound for Rubery passes 516 on service 72 which was the short-working service number for journeys to or from Longbridge only.

Cam took surprisingly few 1952 pictures on the Bristol Road; Maybe he considered that he had covered it adequately pre-war or simply that everybody else was recording these routes in 1952. In these two views which have only superficial changes today, tram 762 **(above)** from City is setting down passengers in Bournbrook at the Dawlish Road stop and **(below)** the railway bridge at Selly Oak station leaves no doubt where this picture was taken although the advertisement has altered and there is now overhead wiring on the railway instead of on the roadway. 762 (again) climbs up from Bournbrook on its way to Rubery.

Above: After traversing the busy section of Selly Oak, car 779 kicks up the dust on a Rednal service as it regains the dual carriageway shortly before Weoley Park Road. The notice board behind the parked Morris Minor identifies the exact spot as it marks the Society of Friends Meeting House, still there today.

Below: At Longbridge, Bristol Road South narrowed to cross the River Rea and a railway line. The building on the left was a railway parcels and advance booking office but did not cater for the adjoining station which was used by workmen's services only.

807 on service 71 will turn right for Rubery once the point cleaner has finished his work and meanwhile waits well back so that the driver does not operate the points while they are being cleaned. The skate to actuate the points can be seen in the overhead just in advance of the trolley pole of 807. Behind is car 810 destined for Rednal on service 70 while 520 recedes into the distance on a Rubery to City journey.

When the bridge was being widened in 1924/5, the trams ran on temporary tracks on the east side. Although the lines from Longbridge to Rednal and to Rubery were constructed as part of the same contract, the Rubery branch lay unused for almost eighteen months because it could not easily be connected at the spot seen in this picture until the tracks were in their final position once the bridge rebuilding was complete.

Above: The first section of tramway in Birmingham to be placed on a central reservation was in Pebble Mill Road, brought into use on 12th October 1919. Here we are looking down from Bristol Road towards Pershore Road. In order to free space in Selly Oak depot during conversion work for buses, a number of trams were outstabled here from 3rd September 1951 requiring the introduction of single-line working. Crossovers were installed and the signal lights were purchased second-hand from the Sheffield Transport Department. In this early 1952 picture, 528 heads the line-up.

Below: Later in 1952, looking south in Pershore Road, car 830 passes Kitchener Road. The gable end behind the tram is on the corner of Hobson Road and the sign advertises "Bob's Café"; largely unchanged in 2007, the premises now house Lesley's Corner Café. The picture was taken to record the kink in the tram lines and particularly the uncommon "tram pinch" road sign on the extreme left which was to warn motorists driving alongside trams on their nearside, although Cam's Austin A40 would have prevented any such manoeuvre at the time of the photo. The kink was a relic of the alteration of the track from single to double line in 1914, combined with road widening at a later date.

At Dogpool Lane, Pershore Road became, and still remains, rather narrow. As 816 approaches **(above)**, we are looking south, with St Stephen's Road on the right and the *Dogpool Hotel* (now the *Hibernian*) on the corner but the off-licence across the road has long since been demolished. The road from here to Warwards Lane was only 22 feet wide between kerbs, too narrow for double track so single line with one intermediate passing loop remained until the route was abandoned in 1952. Car 803 **(below)** unloads in the loop as one of Allenways two distinctive half-deck Foden coaches seizes the opportunity to pass. Looking north this time, the *Hibernian* is seen from the other end. The position of the loop is today marked by the junction with a new side road named Ten Acres End.

Cam's coverage of Pershore Road makes up for any deficiencies on the main Bristol Road routes, maybe because some other enthusiasts saw the Cotteridge route as less interesting. Right from the construction of the tramways in 1904, the inward route followed Hazelwell Street leaving only the outward line in Pershore Road at this point, though formal one-way systems for all traffic only came many years later. At the southern end of Hazelwell Street, 797 **(above)** exchanges a good load of passengers at the British Oak stop (the pub itself is off picture just behind Quiney's shop. Taken from the same spot but facing south **(below)**, 804 approaches from Cotteridge; the junction on the left of the tram is Hunts Road. The few peak period short workings to British Oak were numbered 46 and reversed on the crossover in the foreground.

Above: In our last 1952 picture on Pershore Road, St Agnes Church on the left will identify the position of this view of Cotteridge tram terminus. 827 is the third of three trams waiting to enter the terminal stub when the occupant thereof moves off to City.

Below: A final picture of one of the Cotteridge depot 812 class cars, in Stratford Road looking from city at the "Camp Hill line" railway bridge which, apart from losing its advertisements, looks much the same today. When the Bristol Road routes closed, a number of cars were temporarily stored at Kyotts Lake Road works until there was room at Witton depot where they were to be broken up. Early in August 1952, withdrawn car 837 is being transferred from the works to Witton for scrapping.

Opposite lower: Outside the turreted building in our back cover view, there was a crossover at Weaman Street (on the left in this picture) where the timekeeper would often instruct particular trams to turn back in order to keep the peak service moving. In this 1953 picture, we see 682 doing just that, with the conductor still stowing the trolley rope. When trams were leaving the terminus fully laden, this turnback procedure also helped to provide empty trams for passengers waiting down the route.

Above: Steelhouse Lane queue barriers and kerbside loading as intending passengers saw it when they went to board their tram. On the left was the Wesleyan and General Assurance Society, an organization which had been most intractable over the years as regards the trams. They had resisted the removal of the tram track from the centre of the road to provide kerbside loading and they resisted the erection of loading barriers, claiming that the pavement would become too restricted. They lost those two battles but their objection to the provision of shelters was sustained so that intending passengers waiting here never gained any protection from the elements. A more general view appears on the back cover.

Above: Aston Road is in the background and 665 is turning from the main road to reach Miller Street depot. On the right, Cam's A40 is once more in the picture. There was quite a sharp curve off the main road into what is actually the end of Aston Brook Street before this second sharp curve into Miller Street. Depending on the angle of the drivers' mirrors, it was possible for the mirror at the rear end of a tram travelling into city to touch the equivalent mirror of a tram making this turn into Aston Brook Street. As actual breakage of mirror and vestibule glass resulted on only one known occasion, no corrective action was deemed necessary.

Today the main road is at a much higher level as it climbs to Dartmouth Circus so almost all of this scene is now lost but, surprisingly, the large detached property behind the tram survives unchanged. A doctor's surgery when the picture was taken, it is now occupied by a company marketing shopfittings and display equipment.

Opposite lower: Aston Station bridge on Lichfield Road in July 1949, taken from the open front balcony of a tram. Approaching car 696 bound for Steelhouse Lane demonstrates how the trolley poles had to swing out to provide clearance under the railway bridge. It is followed by 715 bound for Villa Road on service 5. The entrance to Aston station on the left is very different but under the bridge the *Swan and Mitre* public house on the corner of Holborn Hill looks just the same at the time of writing.

The railway bridge here was originally a brick arch one which had insufficient clearance for double-deck electric cars. It was replaced by the girder bridge seen here at the request and expense of Aston Manor Borough Council. In addition to paying the cost, the council had to pay the railway company £10 a year as a contribution towards the extra costs of painting and maintaining the bridge. After withdrawal of the trams in 1953, negotiations with British Railways led to Birmingham reaching agreement that the annual charge should be cancelled on payment of a one-off capital sum of £235. More recently, road widening has required the bridge to be renewed again.

Above: Cars 331 and 629 are shown here on 8th August 1949 at the junction of Victoria Road (to the left) and Lichfield Road. Cam has managed to record two trams, both on the Lozells service 5 which joined the main Lichfield Road services at this point; though he would no doubt have preferred the absence of the following motorist. The house on the right was a doctor's surgery and although not obvious in this photograph it still showed in its replacement brickwork the repairs which had been made after car 329 got out of control descending Victoria Road and overturned against the building in November 1915.

A selection of views (here and opposite) at Salford Bridge where the Lichfield Road routes diverged to serve Short Heath, Erdington or Pype Hayes. In Lichfield Road the line between Aston Hall Road and Salford Bridge had been moved onto a central reservation in 1922 and the bridge itself was widened in 1926. This left a short section of tramway in Gravelly Hill, north of the bridge, in the middle of a wide road where paving to make a loading station was provided although it took another ten years for shelters to be added. 569 **(above)** loads for Erdington (though the number blind has been interfered with) and 634 is running in to Miller Street depot. Shortly afterwards **(below)** tram 667 leaves for Short Heath followed by another car on the same service as 705 completes the turn from Tyburn Road on its journey from Fort Dunlop to Steelhouse Lane. The trolley pole of 667 is about to pass under the skate to set the points for Gravelly Hill or Slade Road as appropriate.

The whole of this area has now disappeared under the M6 and its connections at Spaghetti Junction. 571 **(above)** leaves for Short Heath with the conductress giving a rather half-hearted hand signal to indicate that her tram is about to turn left into Slade Road. A few minutes later **(below)**, the traffic flowing in all directions seems to be coping very well despite the absence of the point duty policeman and even a brave pedestrian takes the shortest route to his destination. An Erdington tram follows Midland Red's 3407 of Sutton garage on the Birmingham and Burton service 112, a route which remained basically unaltered until finally withdrawn by Arriva in March 2007.

The Stockland Green route (pictured here and opposite), opened in 1912, was constructed under powers obtained by Erdington Urban District Council before incorporation into Birmingham. The extension along Streetly Road followed in 1926.

Above: Shortly after turning off Gravelly Hill, 579 passes under the Sutton Coldfield railway line in Slade Road. When the trams were about to be withdrawn, this bridge became the source of some local concern as to the danger of two buses meeting so single line working was introduced controlled by traffic lights and the pavement widened. After some years, a separate pedestrian tunnel was bored through the embankment, the roadway restored to full use and the traffic lights removed.

Below: 634 has just reached the top of Slade Road at Stockland Green, bound for Short Heath terminus and the crossover for short journeys to this point can just be seen behind the tramcar.

Short Heath terminus looking towards City **(above)** with car 719 approaching. Notice the prefabricated houses – "prefabs" as they were generally known – which were erected immediately after the war to provide urgently needed additional housing. Designed for a ten-year life, in most places they survived for very much longer. Much later, the central reservation was used for one of West Midland PTE's weirder experiments when it was concreted to provide a guided busway. It was provided to show what could be done in a more appropriate location and was certainly of no benefit here. Taken from the same spot but facing the other way, 578 **(below)** stands in the terminal stub. The driver is exchanging departure time signals with the next arrival to see who should go first before he leaves on a short-working journey to Aston Cross, hence the service number 60.

The Tyburn Road route to the junction of Holly Lane (seen here and opposite) was constructed mainly for workers at Fort Dunlop and opened in 1920; the extension to Chester Road followed in 1927. When the route opened, the terminus of the Lozells service at Gravelly Hill was immediately moved round the corner into Tyburn Road which is where we see 589 in this 1950 view **(above)**, waiting for time before returning to Lozells. 637 passes on its way from Pype Hayes to Steelhouse Lane. In the 1953 view **(below)**, we are further along Tyburn Road. The bus stop behind Cam's A40 was not in anticipation of the 1953 closure but was used by the Lozells and Dunlop tramway replacement service. 609, 730 and 640 forming a rush-hour procession towards Salford Bridge are about to pass Abbots Road.

Above: Tyburn Road looking from the junction of Holly Lane towards Kingsbury Road. Although the road is still the same width at the time of writing, the reservation and trees have given way to a filter lane for traffic waiting to turn right into Kingsbury Road.

The trams are 672 bound for City, having just passed 546 travelling towards Pype Hayes in this summertime picture taken shortly before the final abandonment in July 1953. Note the bollards which guarded each section of tramway reservation where there was a paved crossing; these showed red lights at night.

Below: Again in 1953, Pype Hayes terminus at the junction of Tyburn Road and Chester Road with the *Bagot Arms* public house in the background. The route was originally a few yards longer but had to be slightly curtailed when the large roundabout was constructed.

Above: A short branch from Tyburn Road was constructed down Holly Lane in 1930 at the request of the Dunlop Rubber Co. Ltd to bring the trams nearer to their factory. The road between the canal bridge and the terminus was a private one owned by Dunlop and this section of tramway was constructed at their expense. The extensive shelters were moved from the previous loading point on Tyburn Road. 565 stands at the shelter while 608 waits to enter the terminus and the Dunlop office block, now demolished, forms the backdrop. Cam's A40 is once again on view, this time apparently complete with chauffeur.

Below: Sutton New Road replaced the High Street Erdington section shown on page 15. Certain morning peak hour journeys on the Erdington service, which turned back at the Barnabas Road crossover, were numbered 64. On Saturday morning 4th July 1953, the last day of tramway operation in Birmingham, 654 was the very last car to perform this duty and is seen here about to cross over and return to City.

Our final 1953 views of the Erdington service are looking north at Chester Road **(above)** as 667 approaches while 668 follows another tram towards the terminus at the boundary between Birmingham and Sutton Coldfield. The roundabout with its wall surmounted by a hedge several times proved a source of surprise to drivers along the Chester Road who encountered a tram coming through the middle of the roundabout and was the scene of some nasty collisions. The widened junction is today controlled by traffic lights. Finally **(below)** at the Erdington terminus the conductress has already alighted from 676 and has the trolley rope in hand ready to turn the trolley pole so that the crew can make a prompt getaway for Miller Street depot. On the original print, the destination “depot only” can be seen. Behind is car 674 waiting for scheduled departure time for City. Originally in the middle of the road, the terminus was moved out of the traffic flow into an area between the main road and a service road in March 1923.

Although Birmingham's last tram service ended on 4th July 1953, there was one further movement yet to come. The final batch of trams was to be broken up Kyotts Lake Road and at Witton but there was insufficient room to accommodate all of them so that eight trams had to remain in Miller Street depot for the time being. Those final eight were moved in the early evening of 7th July 1953. At 8.03pm, the final car to leave was 623 which became the very last tram to travel through the streets of Birmingham, arriving at Witton at 8.15pm. Cam has no photograph of 623 on the move because, very fittingly, he was an invited passenger on it but his picture of it awaiting departure from Miller Street is an excellent study of the platform and bogie detail of the tram. On the platform, the Transport Department's Chief Engineer William Goodall-Copestake (left) and Assistant Chief Engineer Henry Robinson pose for the camera.

Above: No sooner had the trams gone, than the need arose for Cam to record some threatened bus services. The Corporation had announced their intention to discontinue some of the most unremunerative routes and also to split the comparatively few cross-city services at the city centre. This is Station Street, which we have illustrated earlier, with New Street Station behind the buses and the back of the *Futurist* cinema beyond. In earlier times, it was the prime City terminus for Coventry Road and Stratford Road services but as the business and shopping centre of Birmingham moved further north, the alternative Albert Street terminus gained in popularity and by the time this photograph was taken both the services seen here operated at peak hours only.

On 22nd July 1953, buses 1976 and 2897 provide an excellent contrast between the older traditional Birmingham bus and later vehicles. The obvious contrast is between the exposed radiator of the older vehicle with the concealed radiator of the later but note also the half-drop saloon windows on 1976 have given way to sliding ventilators on 2897.

In fact, the Licensing Authority for the West Midland Traffic Area refused the Corporation's application on the grounds that it would mean a sharp increase in fares for some passengers which, in their view, could not be justified so these routes lingered on until last running on 16th August 1958 (46 to Hall Green) or 31st March 1961 (57B to Yardley).

Above: Service 36 ran between Station Street and Stechford via Sparkbrook and this is the outer terminus in Richmond Road on 22nd July 1953. As it was only proposed to withdraw the section between City and Sparkbrook, services at this point would have been unaltered but maybe Cam was unaware of this at the time. That curtailment eventually took effect from 21st September 1958. On the right is one of the wartime "utility" shelters erected in a nationwide programme from 1943 in order to provide cover at strategic points for workers at a time when reduced services meant that they might have lengthy waits. The batch of buses 1844 to 1880 went new to Highgate Road garage which was responsible for the 36 service. Note that the second bus (1867) has the original style of destination blind as supplied by the bodybuilder, the most obvious point being the distinctive numbers with flat-topped "3". In the foreground, 1852 has a replacement destination blind of more traditional Birmingham style.
Below: The 1A service was not to be withdrawn so presumably Cam just fancied to record one of the small batch of fifteen AEC buses with distinctive Park Royal bodies, also on 22nd July 1953. This is Stratford Road just north of the bridge over the River Cole. 1641 has left Acocks Green and will turn up College Road to run via Edgbaston to the City. The pre-war Midland Red bus following on a service from Shirley or points further afield will take the more direct route along Stratford Road to the Bull Ring.

Our final views on 22nd July 1953 depict the two Hall Green and Kingstanding cross-city services. Under the proposed cuts (see page 95), the 29A service would have been split and the 29 withdrawn entirely south of the city centre. Crossley 2375 of Perry Barr garage **(above)** turns through the dual carriageway in Highfield Road at the Yardley Wood Station terminus of service 29. Our final view **(below)** is the end of the evening rush hour at the Hall Green terminus of the 29A at *The Baldwin.* Of the three Daimlers, two are Yardley Wood garage buses, 2858 returning to Pheasey Estate and 2836 running into garage. Behind them is 1860 of Highgate Road garage which has worked a rush hour service from Camp Hill and is also now bound for its garage.

Above: Barford Street garage shortly before closure. 1948 Daimlers 1621, 1623 and 1630 are visible. The garage was opened on 10th June 1925 and closed after service on 16th April 1955. It only accommodated 36 buses and it can be seen that access was somewhat limited. When Lea Hall garage opened on 17th April 1955 it took over some Liverpool Street workings and the Barford Street duties were consequently transferred to Liverpool Street. Transferred to the Police Department in 1955, the exterior appearance of the building is unchanged in 2007; it is currently occupied by Express Polythene Ltd.

Below: Midland Red 1931 stands in Bearwood Bus Station on 14th August 1955 before taking up service on route 213 to Handsworth (New Inns). It is one of a series of views taken at Bearwood on this date and, for once, we cannot trace any special reason. However, 1931 was withdrawn only six weeks later on 30th September 1955 so Cam has fortuitously captured yet another imminent demise.

Above: A Lichfield City to Birmingham New Street train calls at Four Oaks station behind this 2-6-4T locomotive 42470. We cannot date this picture accurately more than to say the 1950s. The service to Four Oaks was dieselized in March 1956 but some of the Lichfield services remained steam-hauled for some time afterwards. The carriage sidings on the right have long since gone and the site, for many years occupied by a builders' merchant, is, at the time of writing, intended to be redeveloped with apartments.

Below: Winson Green station, as one of the early lightweight diesel units approaches on a local service from Wolverhampton High Level to Birmingham New Street. The station closed on 16th September 1957 and this photograph was taken shortly before. The main line is on the left whilst the tracks on the right lead to Soho East Junction and Handsworth Wood, the actual junction being behind the camera. When the line was electrified the junction was moved westward and the four tracks were reduced to two so that one line could pass under each bridge arch, avoiding the need for raising the roadway to accommodate the overhead catenary.

Services 20 and 20B both ran between City and Selly Oak via Harborne, the only difference between them being their routes through the Weoley Castle Estate. These services were to be revised from 21st July 1957 and use of the number 20 discontinued, hence these views. Looking down Chapel Lane, Selly Oak, almost from the corner of Bristol Road **(above)** all the buildings have now gone. Standing at the terminus are Daimlers 1572, 2804 and 1576 and Cam has accidentally captured an unusual working as the time is 5.48pm and 2804 which arrived on service 20 is displaying "Navigation Street" because it will return to City on the Bristol Road 62 route. The 16 minute journey time, compared with 40 minutes via the usual route, will allow the bus to make another peak journey on 20B at 6.04pm from City. The city terminus was in Suffolk Street just above Navigation Street where Daimler 1575 **(below)** awaits departure time. The impressive building behind the bus is the Central Grammar School where Cam was once a pupil. Later known as the Central Technical School, it was demolished when Suffolk Street was widened to become Suffolk Street Queensway.

The Weoley Castle revisions mentioned opposite required new destination blinds for Harborne garage so the opportunity was taken to alter other Harborne service numbers in line with the current policy (suffix letters for short workings but none for main route numbers). Service 2B, which ran between Ivy Bush and Kings Heath, was to be renumbered 2. At the Ivy Bush, buses **(above)** terminated in Vicarage Road Edgbaston, departing via Chad Road. Daimler 1537 from Birmingham's first batch of post-war buses waits for time. The distinguished building on the left remains; the garage with open doors has been converted to a room but otherwise there is little external alteration to what are now offices occupied by National Express. Our other view **(below)** is in Dawlish Road Bournbrook and the main Bristol Road crosses behind the buses. Daimler 2814 is at its terminus and is bound for Kings Heath. Across the road 2808 loads on service 2B for the Ivy Bush. Service 26 between Kings Heath and Bournbrook pre-dated the 2 and became a short working of it when the 2B started on 1st January 1939. The new policy would see the number 26 discontinued – journeys terminating at the point would then rather confusingly become 2B.

Above: Taken in 1953 or 1954, Midland Red 1791 has just breasted the brow of the hill to cross the Tame Valley Canal in Walsall Road bound for Beeches Estate on service 188. By then it was one of the oldest double-deck vehicles remaining in the Midland Red fleet, being new in January 1936 and shortly to be withdrawn in October 1954.

Below: There had been discussions for some years about the Corporation taking over the Great Barr and Beeches Estate services operated for them by the Midland Red company. However, it was not until 1st September 1957 that the Beeches service was transferred from Midland Red and these pictures were taken shortly before. At the City terminus in New Street, 4519 loads for Walsall whilst 4516 inconveniences a taxi while it double banks waiting to get onto its own loading point. The distinctive "Odeon" sign is partly visible above the Walsall bus with the Arden Hotel and the imposing Lloyds Bank Chambers beyond that. Above the taxi, temporary buildings including a Milk Bar can be seen; these had replaced bomb damaged buildings between Worcester Street and High Street, virtually the site of the present Rotunda.

In two more 1957 photographs, we see **(above)** 4457 loading for Beeches Estate in Walsall Road, Perry Barr. The brow of the road in the distance marks the bridge over the railway at Perry Barr Station. The spire of Christ Church is visible on the left but that building had already become a timber merchant's by this date. The coaches on the right have perhaps brought passengers to the Perry Barr Greyhound Racing Stadium whose entrance was alongside. This area was one of the possibilities considered for the relocation of the Perry Barr tram terminus which we mentioned on page 14. Further from town, **(below)** 2336 of 1939 vintage turns from Thornbridge Avenue into Beeches Road returning to New Street from Beeches Estate. The view along Beeches Road to the left of the bus is nowadays dominated by the viaduct of the M6 crossing.

Above: In the course of a review of the Transport Department's operations, it was suggested that limited stop services should be tried and with some obvious reluctance, a service 99 was experimentally introduced on 16th February 1959 as an evening peak limited stop version of the 14 between City and Tile Cross, It started from a separate terminus in James Watt Street and was limited stop as far as Stechford Lane. The running time was six minutes less than on the 14 but in practice congestion at Saltley often nullified any benefit. The buses concerned were drawn from the 14 service, which reduced frequency on that route and this brought complaints from the platform staff that those buses were excessively busy whilst some of the limited stop services were lightly laden. The Transport Committee decided that the experiment should not be extended and the 99 last ran on 15th May 1959. The service was restricted to the newer "triple indicator" equipped vehicles so that destination blinds did not need to be specially printed. 2751 is at Tile Cross with older Daimler 1605 on the ordinary service.

Left: Tipton Five Ways station looking north with 4594 arriving on a Wolverhampton to Stourbridge local. A typical Camwell shot including station name board but we can find no obvious reason for the view and it seems an unlikely location for Cam to have been on a casual visit. The station closed on 30th July 1962 but the view must pre-date November 1960 when the locomotive was withdrawn from service.

Above: Locomotive 58271 at Longbridge on another rail tour on 30th May 1959, this one to commemorate the Golden Jubilee of the Stephenson Locomotive Society. The tour had just arrived from Halesowen. We are looking west from the footbridge connecting the platforms which were used for Austin Works services; the present Longbridge station on the main line did not then exist. Quite apart from the novelty of having a very old locomotive on the tour, dating from 1896, severe weight restrictions on Hunnington viaduct meant that there were not many other types of suitable engine which could be used on the branch.

Below: The original reversing manoeuvre at Hamstead terminus was simply to turn round in the junction of Hamstead Road and Old Walsall Road. As traffic levels grew this became undesirable and eventually a turning bay was constructed just in Hamstead Road, as seen here, and was brought into use on 10th December 1961. Shortly afterwards, bus 1904 was photographed as it departed for Yardley via the city centre on service 15, one of Birmingham's few cross-city routes; journeys in the reverse direction were numbered 16. The chimney and pithead gear are part of Hamstead Colliery.

Engineering work on the West Coast Main Line between Rugby and Stafford often brought diversions through Birmingham as they still do today. At Aston station **(above)** one Sunday in 1962, Jubilee class 4-6-0 45672 *Anson* passes through on a diverted West Coast service to London Euston. The signals near the signal box mark the junction for Witton and Bescot straight ahead, or branching right for Gravelly Hill and the Lichfield line. Behind the photographer is another junction where the train will bear left for Stechford and Coventry, rather than right for New Street. On the same date but taken from the bridge which now leads to Sandwell Valley nature centre **(below)**, a Class 40 diesel hauls the 0950 Euston to Blackpool Central; Hamstead Colliery can be seen in the background.

Above: Photographed at New Street on 2nd June 1962, 0-8-0 48930 works yet another special tour which Cam had organized, the excuse for this one being to commemorate the centenary of the opening of the Sutton Coldfield line. The locomotive was almost sixty years old, being built in April 1903 by the London & North Western Railway as part of their Class "D". They were reclassified officially as G2A when the original saturated-steam boilers had been replaced by superheated ones but were invariably known to railwaymen and enthusiasts alike as "Super D".
Below: An empty stock train hauled by Class 5 4-6-0 45189 passes Handsworth Junction from the Great Barr direction, heading towards Soho. The line diverging to the right leads to Perry Barr and this triangle of lines is still in use today. The signal box closed on 5th July 1966 when its functions were absorbed into Birmingham power box control and on the same date Handsworth Junction was renamed Perry Barr West Junction to avoid confusion with the nearby ex-Great Western Handsworth junction (pictured on page 109), by then under the same area management.

Above: Although not a great student of signalboxes Cam was always concerned to record anything which might be about to disappear, especially when it was on his doorstep, so to speak. This is Great Barr signalbox, which was just west of the Old Walsall Road overbridge, taken in 1964. As well as passing traffic, the box controlled both entry to the goods yard and the ground frame giving access to Hamstead Colliery a few hundred yards west. The goods station closed on 1st June 1964 and the colliery in March 1965. The signal box gained a short period of glory when it became the fringe box working to the new Walsall power signal box from 6th December 1965 but it closed on 3rd July 1966, when the area controlled by New Street power signal box was extended to meet the Walsall box area.

Below: Sutton Park station looking west, as a diesel unit calls on the infrequent Walsall to Birmingham service, shortly before the service was withdrawn on 18th January 1965.

Above: There must have been a specific purpose for this view for Cam to have taken the trouble to reach this somewhat inaccessible vantage point, perhaps to record one of the remaining steam hauled services when most had turned over to diesel units. Taken either in 1963 or 1964, 2-6-2T locomotive 4158 is hauling a Birmingham to Wolverhampton service at Handsworth Junction. The line on the right leads to Stourbridge and is in use today but the route the train is taking is now the line of the Midland Metro. The overbridge marks Halfords Lane and The Hawthorns metro station is now just beyond.

Below: At New Street station, late in 1965, the new Birmingham power signal box is visible above the bridge on the left but will not be brought into use until 10th January 1966. New Street No.5 signal box seen here is still controlling the trains at this end of the station. The signal on the right in the foreground was the last semaphore signal surviving at New Street from London & North Western Railway days and the photo was taken specifically to record this, while Cam's old school still forms a backdrop.

When the North Warwickshire railway line between Tyseley and Bearley was proposed for closure, there was considerable opposition mainly based on the inadequacy of the planned replacement buses and it was several years before the proposal was finally dropped. The details are too long to recount here but on 27th July 1968, Cam decided to record the scene **(above)** at Hall Green station looking towards Tyseley. The destination blind shows "Special" but this was probably an ordinary local service as rear blinds often failed to be adjusted in those days. In the driver's window, a board with the number 304 records the "set number" allocated to this Class 116 diesel unit by Tyseley depot where it was based. A little further out of town **(below)** similar set 319 on the 1445 Henley-in-Arden to Moor Street calls at Whitlocks End. This class was built at Derby in 1957 and ran most of the ex-Western Region services around Birmingham.

Above: On 7th September 1968, the 1625 Wolverhampton Low Level to Birmingham Snow Hill service calls at West Bromwich. After a reduction to peak journeys only, the line was finally closed on 6th March 1972, the station building having been demolished some time before. The overbridge in the background is Lyng Lane which is now divertcd to run into Moor Street; West Bromwich Metro station now stands on this site. The single-unit Class 122 diesel car 55009, was built in 1958 by the Gloucester Railway Carriage & Wagon Co. Ltd. This particular railcar survived a visit to the scrap dealer and is now preserved on the North Norfolk Railway.
Below: On 2nd August 1973, a class 304 e.m.u. on the 0920 from Walsall runs in to Birmingham New Street passing class 52 diesel 1015 *Western Champion* which has arrived with the 0653 from Paddington. This was one of the last booked "Western" duties into Birmingham and no doubt the reason for the picture. Headcode 1V28 indicates that the locomotive will return to Paddington on the 1025 departure.

The last word: In a characteristic pose, Cam patiently awaits the photographer's attention, having allowed his camera to be used by someone else. The train is at Harborne station on 3rd June 1950 on the occasion of the first of many Rail Tours organized by Cam over freight-only lines or routes under threat of closure. Appropriately this first tour covered the line where Cam's earliest Birmingham photographs had been taken nearly 16 years before (see page 7). The tour was accompanied by BBC and press representatives and was mentioned on that evening's regional news. The success of this tour undoubtedly was the spur for all those which followed, despite the many difficulties which were involved in their organization, even in those days when British Railways was a single entity. A ticket issued for that first tour is illustrated below.

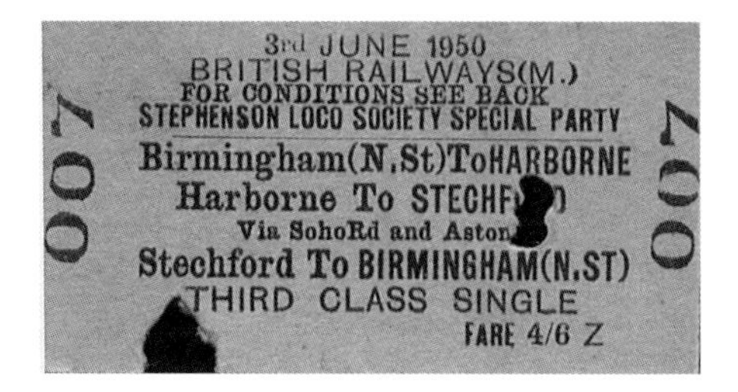

Printed and bound by Gomer Press Ltd, Llandysul, SA44 4JL